# Betty Crocker's
# Kitchen Secrets

# Betty Crocker's
# Kitchen Secrets

Random House, Inc. New York

Library of Congress Cataloging in Publication Data   Crocker, Betty. Betty Crocker's Kitchen Secrets.

Includes index.   1. Cookery.   I. Title.   II. Title: Kitchen Secrets.
TX651.C76   1983   641.5   82-48962   ISBN 0-394-52306-7

Manufactured in the United States of America          24689753          First Edition

# Foreword

If you are a beginning cook or if you have cooked for years but would like an authoritative, up-to-date refresher course or the answer to a particular cooking problem, this book is for you.

We believe that good cooks are made, not born, and that successful results come from doing the right things in the best ways, every time. Here are what we have found to be the best ways, developed through years of experience and practice in the Betty Crocker Kitchens.

This is not a recipe book. Nor is it a collection of miscellaneous, quick kitchen tips. All of the information, techniques and "secrets" contained here have been carefully tested, authenticated and practiced in the Betty Crocker Kitchens to give you the confidence you need in your own kitchen.

Whether you consult *Betty Crocker's Kitchen Secrets* as an excellent kitchen reference guide or read it cover to cover for all the fascinating facts it contains, you will find that its clear, everyday language and hundreds of how-to sketches and color photographs are like having a home economics consultant right at your elbow as you cook.

*Betty Crocker's Kitchen Secrets* begins with a section filled with new and time-tested techniques and tips — the kind of helps that are rarely found in recipes. They are fully illustrated and augmented with easy-to-read charts that explain basic ingredients, baking and cooking methods together with generic cooking terms.

Interspersed are hundreds of answers to the most-often-asked cooking questions and problems that occur in kitchens.

The second section is devoted to guidelines for cooking and baking, including cooking at high altitudes, measuring ingredients, yields and equivalents. It gives recommendations for the selection and multiple uses of equipment, appliances, bakeware and utensils — both the basics and those not essential but nice to have. It details secrets of selecting food in more than 100 categories and tells how to save money while purchasing quality foods as well as how to store them successfully and safely.

Here in one convenient volume are the secrets and techniques of the Betty Crocker Kitchens to use with all your favorite recipes. *Betty Crocker's Kitchen Secrets* is a valuable, timely addition to your kitchen bookshelf and a gift that any new cook among your friends or family would be grateful to receive.

*Betty Crocker*

# Contents

# Tips & Techniques

## Beverages • 12

## Breads, Quick • 19

## Breads, Yeast • 25

## Cakes & Frostings • 30

## Candy • 36

## Chocolate Flavoring • 37

## Condiments • 38

## Cookies • 40

# Dairy Foods · 44

Cheese 44 · Cream 46 · Milk 46 · Sour Cream 46 · Yogurt 46

# Desserts · 47

# Eggs · 50

# Fats & Oils · 52

# Flours · 53

# Fruits · 54

Apples to Watermelons

# Garnishes · 62

Butter, Cheese and Egg 62 · Fruit 62 · Vegetable 63

# Grains · 64

# Herbs, Seeds & Spices · 65

Allspice to Turmeric 65 · Growing Herbs 70

# Legumes · 72

# Marinades · 74

# Meats · 75

Selecting and Cooking 76 · General Cooking Methods 82 ·
Carving 84

# Kitchen Guidelines

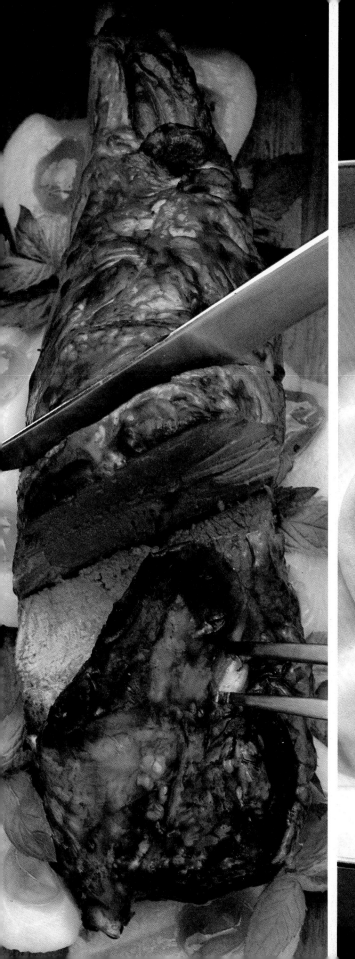

# Tips & Techniques

# Beverages

Here are the secrets of making really delicious coffee for a crowd,
flaming glamorous desserts, preventing an opened bottle of wine from going sour
and brewing crystal clear — never cloudy — iced tea.

## Coffee

### Ground Coffee

**Regular** grind is an intermediate grind size used in automatic percolator-type coffee makers and range-top percolators.

**Drip** or fine grind is used in drip coffee makers and espresso machines in which the water passes through the grounds only once.

**Special** grinds — electric perk and flaked — are designed especially for electric percolators and automatic drip coffee makers.

### Decaffeinated Coffee

Most of the caffeine has been removed through steaming and treatment with solvents. Some of the aroma and flavor of pure ground coffee is lost in the process.

### Instant Coffee

Pure ground coffee is brewed and the water evaporated, leaving a fine powder called instant coffee. Sometimes the ground coffee is brewed, frozen into slabs, then ground and dried to a granular form of instant coffee called freeze-dried.

### Special Coffees

Coffee is the essential ingredient in a variety of beverages served in special classic combinations. Café au lait, for example, is popular in France as a breakfast beverage. It is a combination (usually equal parts) of hot coffee and hot milk poured simultaneously into the cup from 2 pots, one held in each hand. Irish coffee can follow or replace the dessert course at dinner. It is a mixture of Irish whiskey and sugar stirred into hot coffee and topped with heavy or whipped cream. Spiced coffee is made by adding spices, citrus peel and sugar to coffee and is served between or with meals.

### Problems and Solutions

☐ *How do I clean the coffeepot?*

Clean all coffeepots after each use with hot, soapy water and rinse well with hot water. Occasionally clean metal parts and all hard-to-reach places with a brush or pipe cleaner. A chemical coffee-maker cleanser can be used occasionally in metal percolators.

☐ *How do I make the perfect cup of coffee?*

The strength of coffee is determined by the ratio of coffee to water during brewing. Depending on personal taste, 1 to 3 tablespoons coffee should be used for each ¾ cup water. Always use fresh cold water in a thoroughly clean coffee maker because hot water may contain mineral deposits from water pipes that can affect the flavor of the coffee, and oils from brewed coffee remaining in a pot can contribute an undesirable bitterness. Serve coffee immediately after brewing or within one hour for peak flavor. Coffee loses aroma and develops a bitter flavor during longer standing or after reheating.

□ *How do I store roasted whole coffee beans?*

Store them in an airtight container to retain aroma. The beans can be frozen, then ground unthawed for an exceptionally fresh-tasting cup of coffee.

□ *How do I store ground coffee?*

Ground coffee that has been opened should be stored in a tightly covered container in the refrigerator to eliminate heat and moisture which cause coffee to lose flavor and become stale. Coffee can also be stored in the freezer.

□ *How do I make coffee for a crowd?*

Measure regular-grind coffee into a clean cloth bag, filling only about ½ full to allow coffee to expand and water to circulate through grounds.

Tie top of bag, leaving enough cord to fasten bag to handle of large container.

Measure cold water into container and heat to full boil; reduce heat.

Submerge bag of coffee in water. Brew, pushing bag up and down with wooden spoon for proper extraction, 6 to 8 minutes.

Remove bag; keep coffee hot but do not allow it to boil.

| **Coffee for a Crowd** | | |
|---|---|---|
| Servings (¾ cup each) | Regular-Grind Coffee | Water |
| 23 | 2 cups | 4 quarts |
| 46 | 4 cups | 8 quarts |
| 100 | 9 cups | 4½ gallons |

□ *How do I make instant coffee for a crowd?*

| **Instant Coffee for a Crowd** | | |
|---|---|---|
| Servings (¾ cup each) | Instant Coffee | Water |
| 25 | 1 cup (2-oz. jar) | 1 gallon |
| 75 | 3½ cups (6-oz. jar) | 3 gallons |
| 125 | 5½ cups (10-oz. jar) | 5 gallons |

Measure instant coffee into a large container. Stir in part of water to dissolve coffee. Add remaining water and bring just to a boil. Keep coffee hot but do not boil.

## Malt Beverages

The most common of the malt-type liquor beverages is beer. Beer may be light and golden or heavy and dark, consumed as a beverage or used in cooking, as in sauerbraten or beer-cheese soup, and marinades. Today's beers, which vary in alcoholic and caloric content, are made from malted barley and other cereals and flavored with hops.

## Milk (See Dairy Foods, page 46)

# Spirits

We think first of spirits in a cocktail or as an after-dinner cordial — seldom as an ingredient in food. While the fine art of cooking with distilled liquors is not for everyday, spirits give subtle flavor to seafood and chicken dishes, game and even vegetables. And what would cherries jubilee or crêpes suzette be without them? Consult the chart on the following page for the many uses of spirits in food.

**Brandy** is a distillation of wine and is consumed as a liqueur as well as a spirit.

**Liqueur** is alcohol which has been flavored with extracts from flowers, fruits and herbs; with fruits and herbs; or with just fruits. It is usually sweetened with honey or syrups.

**Rum** is a distillation of sugarcane or molasses and is consumed in cocktails, or on ice with or without soda or tonic.

**Whiskey** is a distillation of a variety of grains. The manufacturer and the ingredients determine the differences among whiskeys.

## Problems and Solutions

□ *What does "proof" mean in liquor?*

Proof stands for the minimum alcoholic strength of a liquor with reference to the arbitrary standard for spirits. For example, the designation "100 proof" means that the liquor is 50 percent alcohol.

□ *What happens when I flame foods?*

Flambéed foods acquire the flavor of liquor without the alcohol because the alcoholic content evaporates as it heats, and only the "essence" is left, to impart its subtle flavor. The spirit used should be 80 proof and its flavor compatible with the food to be flamed. After flaming (pictured at right), stir the food gently to equalize the flavor.

Simple flaming desserts can be made by soaking sugar cubes in lemon, orange, rum or brandy extract, placing cubes around dessert and lighting with a long match.

□ *How do I flame foods?*

**Heat** brandy in small long-handled pan over medium heat just until warm.

**Ignite** brandy, using long match.

**Pour** flaming brandy over fruit. Stir gently.

## Popular Spirits for Cooking or Flavoring Foods

| Spirit | Flavor | Compatible with These Foods |
|---|---|---|
| Amaretto | almond | coffee cakes, desserts, fruit, ice cream |
| Benedictine | brandy, herbs, honey | coffee, desserts, flambéed fruit |
| Brandy, fruit flavored | distilled sweetened fruit wine | fruit, flambéed poultry, sauces |
| Calvados | apple | desserts, game, pork, veal |
| Cognac (brandy) | distilled grape wine | coffee, flambéed fruit and poultry |
| Cointreau, curacao, Triple Sec, Grand Marnier | orange | crepes, fruit salad and soufflés, poultry, pork, seafood, vegetables |
| Crème de banane | banana | desserts |
| Crème de cacao | cocoa, vanilla | desserts, ice cream, mousse |
| Crème de cassis | currant | desserts, ice cream, sherbet |
| Crème de menthe | peppermint | desserts, fruit, ice cream |
| Drambuie | Scotch whiskey, herbs, spices | coffee, ice cream |
| Galliano | herbs, anise | cakes, desserts, fruit |
| Gin | alcohol, juniper berry | game, kidneys |
| Kahlúa | coffee | cakes, coffee, desserts, ice cream |
| Kirsch | cherry | cakes, fruits, flambéed foods |
| Kummel | caraway, fennel | cabbage, sauerkraut, desserts |
| Maraschino | cherry | cakes, desserts, ice cream |
| Peppermint Schnapps | peppermint | desserts, frostings, ice cream |
| Pernod | anise | coffee, seafood |
| Rum | sweet, sugarcane-based | cakes, desserts, rum fruit pot |
| Sambuca | anise | coffee, desserts |
| Strega | herbs | desserts, fruit |
| Tia Maria | coffee, rum, spices | chocolate desserts, ice cream |

# Tea

Here's to tea, the nearly universal symbol of relaxation and sociability. From the afternoon tea of the English to the tea ceremony of the Japanese, the Russian glass of tea and the minted teas of the Middle East, it is a cultural rite with meaning far beyond the American cup of coffee. To us, it offers iced refreshment in a tinkling glass and comfort in a steaming cup. So, know your tea and how to brew it properly.

**Black** tea, most popular in western countries of the world, derives its amber color and aromatic flavor from fermented leaves of the tea plant. The finest-flavored and most expensive teas are grown at high altitudes. The leaves are processed to preserve and concentrate the oils in tea. The name "orange pekoe black tea" indicates the leaf size, not the flavor. Darjeeling black tea is pictured, (1) above.

**Blended** tea is a combination of many grades of teas from many countries and tea estates. Some of the best-known blends are Earl Grey, English Breakfast, (3) above, Russian Style and spiced blends.

**Green** tea, the favorite of the eastern countries of the world, is pale golden green in color. The leaves are steamed and heat-dried. The flavor of green tea is slightly bitter and the lightest color produces the best brew. Gunpowder, (4) above, is a high-grade green tea made from young leaves rolled into small balls.

**Oolong** tea is partially fermented and a cross between green and black teas; it is amber in color and is sometimes flavored with jasmine flowers, (2) above, for a fruity taste. Oolong is grown in China and Taiwan but is also popular in America.

## Problems and Solutions

□ *How do I make a good cup of tea?*

Tea should be made in a clean ceramic teapot because metal pots can affect the delicate flavor of the tea. Heat fresh cold water to a boil. Rinse the teapot with some of the boiling water and drain. Use 1 teaspoon loose tea or 1 tea bag for each cup of tea. Add tea or tea bags to the warm pot and pour boiling water over the tea. Cover and let stand 3 to 5 minutes to steep the tea and bring out the full flavor. Strength of tea is judged by flavor, not by color.

□ *How do I make tea for a crowd?*

Prepare a concentrate by placing ¼ pound (1½ cups) loose tea in a large container and pouring 2½ quarts boiling water over tea; steep 5 minutes. Strain tea leaves. Mix 1 part concentrate to 3 parts boiling water and serve as needed. This concentrate will make about 50 servings of tea.

□ *How do I prevent iced tea from becoming cloudy after it is brewed?*

To make clear tea, place tea and cold water in a glass container. Cover and refrigerate 24 hours. Serve over crushed ice. You also can make strong, clear tea using boiling water. Let cool to room temperature and pour over ice cubes.

# Wine

Wine — sparkling, red, rosé, and white — was once reserved for state occasions and celebrations, a symbol of high living. Today, however, as American-produced wines gain a respected place in world markets, wine appears on many home dining tables almost as a matter of course. We cook with it, we serve it with food and, increasingly, we ask for it in place of cocktails and cordials. We drink it with fruit and cheese and offer it alone as a small, elegant gesture of hospitality. Today, personal tastes, not traditional rules, decree which wine we shall offer with any food. This, then, is all you really need to know to select wines with confidence and serve them with style.

**Fortified** wines include sherry, port and Madeira. All three are fermented wines with a spirit, such as brandy or sugarcane spirit added as a strengthener and preservative. These wines are sweet and strong and last indefinitely at room temperature.

**Red** wines are made from grapes fermented to convert natural sugars to alcohol and carbonic gas. This process takes a few days to many months. Dry red wines are known as Bordeaux, Burgundy, Chianti, claret and others. Medium red wines are known as Catawba red, Lake Country red, Lambrusco and others. Sweet red wines are known as kosher Concord, Malaga, sweet (red) vermouth and others.

**Rosé** wines are made from grapes fermented into alcohol but the coloration is minimized, resulting in a rose-colored wine. Popular dry rosé wines are Gringnolino rosé, Zinfandel rosé, rosé de Provence and others. Medium rosé wines are known as Grenache rosé, rosé d'Anjou and others.

**Sparkling** wines include champagne, pink champagne, cold duck, sparkling Burgundy and Chablis. They are fermented twice to produce a bubbly wine.

**White** wines include dry, medium and sweet. Well-known dry white wines include Chablis, grey Riesling, Pinot Chardonnay, dry (white) vermouth, some kosher wines and others.

Varieties of medium white wines include Liebfraumilch, Rhine, white Anjou and others. Sauterne, muscatel, Tokay, some kosher wines and others like them are sweet white wines.

## Problems and Solutions

☐ *How many servings do various-sized bottles of wine contain?*

| Servings by Wine Bottle Sizes | | | |
|---|---|---|---|
| Bottle Size | Ounces | Dinner Wine Servings | Champagne Servings |
| Split | 6.4 | 1 - 2 | 1 - 2 |
| Fifth | 25.6 | 6 - 8 | 8 |
| Quart | 32 | 8 - 10 | 8 - 10 |
| Magnum | 52 | 16 | 16 |
| Jeroboam | 104 | | 32 |
| Gallon | 128 | 30 - 40 | |
| Rehoboam | 156 | | 48 |

☐ *Which wines are traditionally served with which foods?*

There are many exceptions to the traditional rule of serving white wine with lighter meats, red wines with darker meats and rosé with both kinds. While champagne and rosé wines are traditionally served with many foods, today personal taste can properly dictate choices of wine to accompany any food. You can serve whatever wine you like with whatever food you like.

☐ *At what temperature should I serve wine?*

Red wines are usually served at 60° to 65°F. White wines are usually served at 40° to 50°F. Champagne should be served thoroughly chilled but never below 35°F or it might be damaged. Rosé is usually served at 40° to 50°F.

## ☐ *When cooking with wine, which ones should I use?*

Red wines are used in marinades to tenderize meat and in cooking to bring out the flavor of foods. White wines are used in delicate sauces or diluted with water and used to poach fish. Both red and white wines are usually simmered to disperse the alcohol and mellow the flavor. Inexpensive but drinkable wines should be used for cooking. Food is often best served with the same kind of wine with which it was cooked.

## ☐ *How should I store wine?*

Wine bottles should be stored on their sides so that the corks remain wet and tight. A dark place with a constant temperature of 55°F is best for storage of unopened bottles of wine. Once opened, any leftover wine should be poured into a small bottle that has an airtight top to delay deterioration. White wine should be refrigerated; red wine should be stored at room temperature for 1 to 2 days.

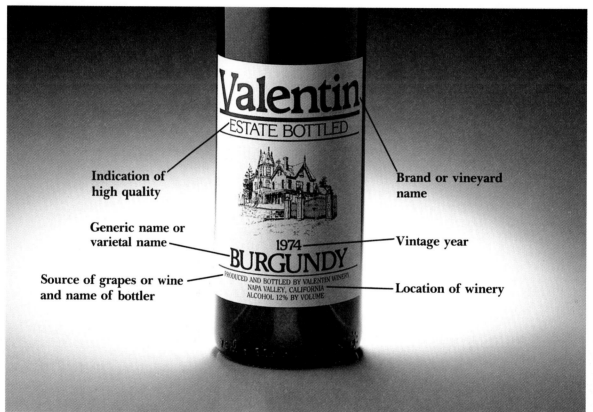

Indication of high quality

Brand or vineyard name

Generic name or varietal name

Vintage year

Source of grapes or wine and name of bottler

Location of winery

## ☐ *How do I read a wine label?*

An American wine label will state the brand or vineyard name and the generic name of the wine. The term "estate bottled" means that all the grapes named came from one vineyard and that the wine was processed there.

A vintage year on the label indicates when the grapes were harvested. "Produced by" means that the vineyard processed, fermented and matured at least 75 percent of the grapes, and "made by" indicates that most of the wine probably was obtained from independent growers and bottled by the vineyard.

A location used in the name shows that at least 75 percent of the grapes came from that place.

A European wine label may offer more information about the maker, the grape and the location. The "Appellation controlée" designation indicates that the wine was made in a specific area in a manner prescribed by the French government.

# Breads, Quick

To win a reputation for really wonderful home cooking, you can learn to make quick breads. They're easy, they're as quick as their name implies and they're economical, too, because most of the ingredients you need come straight from your cupboard shelf. Served with a flourish, warm from oven, griddle or pan, they are sure to impress both family and guests, and they contribute good nutrition and heartiness to the simplest meal.

## Problem and Solution

☐ *What is the difference between quick breads and yeast breads?*

Quick breads (pictured below) are made to rise by the addition of quick-acting baking powder instead of by slower-acting yeast. (Refer to Yeast Breads, page 25.)

## Baking Powder Biscuits

Buttered hot biscuits with jam to surprise the family at Sunday breakfast or golden-crusted strawberry shortcake to impress a special guest — whatever the occasion, whatever you serve, there's something about biscuits that always makes it better. And best of all, biscuits are a boon to the beginning cook because they're easy to bake, both from scratch and from a biscuit baking mix.

## Problems and Solutions

☐ *Why is it necessary to cut in shortening until mixture looks like fine crumbs?*

The tiny lumps of shortening produce a flaky texture throughout the biscuits.

☐ *Why is kneading necessary?*

Kneading distributes ingredients and makes biscuits light. With softer dough of drop biscuits, kneading is not necessary; vigorous stirring is sufficient.

☐ *How can I make biscuits that are equal in height?*

Roll biscuit dough between two wooden sticks that are ½ inch high and 14 inches long. Anyone who works with wood can make a pair.

□ *What are the qualities of a good baking powder biscuit?*

A good baking powder biscuit doubles in size during baking, has a golden brown, tender top with lighter sides, is creamy white inside with thin, flaky layers and is slightly moist with a pleasant taste.

□ *I love hot biscuits, but I don't have a biscuit cutter!*

You can pat the biscuit dough out lightly with floured fingers. Cut biscuits with an opened orange juice can or other narrow can dipped in flour.

□ *What is an easy way to make biscuits?*

Pat the biscuits into a square about ½ inch thick and cut into square biscuits with a long knife dipped in flour. This method also saves the step of rerolling scraps of dough, which may toughen biscuits.

# Coffee Cakes

Coffee cakes spell instant hospitality. Equally welcome at breakfast or brunch, they're perfect for coffee breaks, late evening refreshment or even dessert. And their spicy fragrance as they bake can fill your kitchen with the most delicious aroma. Make one or two good coffee cake recipes the specialties of your house and stir one up whenever company's expected.

## Problems and Solutions

□ *What are the qualities of a good coffee cake?*

A good coffee cake has a tender, golden brown crust or crumbly topping and is tender and light inside with an even texture (medium to small round holes). It is slightly moist and delicate with a slightly sweet, pleasant taste and sometimes contains fruit pieces or nuts or has a streusel topping.

□ *Why are shiny pans needed for coffee cakes?*

Shiny pans that reflect heat are necessary for a golden, delicate and tender crust.

□ *How can I tell when my coffee cake is ready to come out of the oven?*

Follow the doneness test given in the recipe. Usually a wooden pick inserted in the center (or near the center for tube pans) comes out clean when the coffee cake is done.

# Doughnuts

Bring back homemade doughnuts to your family. They're easy and fun to make, and yours, fresh and warm from the fryer, will far outshine those from the most popular doughnut shop. Enjoy a cake or raised doughnut with a glass of ice-cold milk, dunk one in a cup of coffee or set out a bowlful with snapping-crisp red apples or a pitcher of apple cider. That's what American country cooking is all about.

## Problems and Solutions

□ *What kind of a pan should I use for frying my doughnuts?*

Use a deep, heavy pan or deep-fat fryer. The deep pan or fryer provides a high side against which to rest the thermometer and helps prevent spattering. (Be sure the handle of the pan is turned away from you, toward the back of the range.)

□ *What are the signs of a good doughnut?*

A good doughnut is golden brown in color, uniform in shape, has a tender, grease-free crust and slightly moist (not gummy) inside with a slightly spicy, pleasant taste.

□ *Sometimes the oil foams up when I slide a doughnut into it.*

Bits of flour can cause the oil to bubble up. Be sure the pan is deep enough to allow for some foaming; the amount of foaming differs among kinds and brands of oil.

□ *Why are my doughnuts sometimes greasy?*

Oil that is not hot soaks into doughnuts before the crust forms. Watch the temperature of the oil closely, adjusting the heat to maintain temperature of 375°F. Drain the cooked doughnuts on paper towels.

□ *Why are my doughnuts hard?*

You may have overmeasured flour or worked too much flour into the dough as you rolled; measure accurately. Use a cloth-covered board and stockinet-covered rolling pin so that doughnut dough does not pick up extra flour (refer to page 43).

□ *Why are my doughnuts dark on the outside and underdone on the inside?*

The oil may have been too hot, which would have browned the doughnuts on the outsides before they cooked through on the insides. Keep the oil temperature constant at 375°F and cook each doughnut 1½ to 2 minutes on each side.

□ *I can't afford a new bottle of oil every time I make doughnuts!*

You can strain the oil after it cools and use it again. Pour it through a funnel lined with a paper coffee filter or a double layer of cheesecloth into a container that has a tight-fitting cover. Store it in the refrigerator no longer than 6 months.

# Dumplings

Fluffy, cloudlike dumplings are perhaps the homiest of all old-fashioned foods. To serve on a stew, a hearty soup or a fricassee, they can be flavored with parsley, herbs or cheese. And unflavored, they can be delicious with fruit for dessert as well. Fast and easy to make, they can stretch a dish to accommodate extra guests and appease the heartiest appetites.

## Problems and Solutions

☐ *What are the qualities of a good dumpling?*

A good dumpling doubles in size during steaming, is snowy white in color, has a fluffy texture throughout with no brown crust and is tender and slightly moist with a pleasant taste.

☐ *Why is it necessary to heat the stew that goes with dumplings first?*

The stew or vegetables must be boiling because dumplings cook from the heat of the meat below them, which also forms steam above them.

☐ *Why are dumplings always cooked both covered and uncovered?*

They are cooked uncovered for lightness, then covered to cook them through.

# Muffins

Steaming hot and fragrant muffins, nestled in a napkin-lined basket, make something special of a bacon-and-egg breakfast, a lunchtime salad or a hot chili supper. Stirred up quickly and baked at coffee time, they warm the hearts of family and drop-in visitors alike. If you've been disappointed with your homemade muffins, read the tips below.

## Problems and Solutions

☐ *What are the qualities of a good muffin?*

It has a slightly rounded, golden brown, pebbly top with a tender crust. The inside is tender and light with an even texture (medium-size round holes), is slightly moist and delicate and has a rather sweet, pleasant taste.

☐ *Why should the batter be lumpy?*

Muffins need very little mixing — just until the flour is moistened, and if you stir until smooth, they will be overmixed. Don't worry, the lumps will disperse during baking.

☐ *Why should only the bottoms of muffin cups be greased?*

This is necessary for nicely shaped muffins that have no rim around the top edges.

# Nut Breads

Think nut breads when you plan to entertain or want a holiday gift from your kitchen. Bake them in loaves, rounds or miniatures, then slice and serve with softened butter or cream cheese and preserves. Cut them into dainty buttered sandwiches to serve with fruit or chicken salad.

## Problems and Solutions

☐ *What are the qualities of good nut bread?*

A good nut bread has a golden brown, rounded top with (often) a characteristic crack lengthwise on top, a thin, tender crust, fairly moist inside with small, even holes. Fruits and/or nuts are evenly distributed, and the bread has a distinct fruit and/or nut flavor.

☐ *My nut bread crumbles when I slice it!*

Be sure bread is completely cool before you slice it; store nut bread twenty-four hours before slicing. Cut with a sharp, thin-bladed knife, and use a light, sawing motion; don't press down.

# Pancakes

What to serve for breakfast, lunch or supper? Pancakes — flapjacks to crepes — provide the all-purpose answer. Pancakes were invented out of frugality to serve with many foods from meat and vegetables to syrup, fruit and ice cream. They're a kitchen secret for times when you want to serve something elegant or only make a meal from next to nothing.

## Problem and Solution

☐ *When are my pancakes ready to turn?*

Turn pancakes as soon as they are puffed and just as the bubbles begin to break.

☐ *How can I tell when the griddle is hot enough for my pancakes?*

Sprinkle the griddle with a few drops of water. If the bubbles skitter around, the heat is just right for frying.

# Popovers

A spectacular restaurant specialty, popovers are surprisingly easy to make in your own kitchen. Impress your family with their crunchy, golden goodness. Serve steaming hot with butter to accompany soups, meats or salads. Split and fill with scrambled eggs or creamed seafood for a versatile main dish worth remembering.

## Problems and Solutions

□ *What are the qualities of a good popover?*

A good popover is a hollow shell, peaked in an irregular pattern and is deep golden brown on top with a crisp, tender crust and very few thin filaments inside. The interior of the crust is moist and the flavor is mild and pleasant.

□ *Why did my popovers collapse after they were baked?*

Not enough eggs, eggs that are too small or too much liquid in proportion to flour can weaken popovers and cause them to collapse. Too low an oven temperature (refer to page 134) can cause underbaking, which also results in collapsed popovers. Follow specific recipe directions carefully.

# Waffles

If you own a waffle iron, you're never at a loss for a delicious main dish or dessert. Everybody likes crisp, delicate waffles swimming in butter and syrup. Topped with creamed chicken, tuna or vegetables, they're hearty fare. With ice cream and fruit or berries and whipped cream, they're a refreshing year-round dessert.

## Problems and Solutions

□ *What are the qualities of a good waffle?*

A good waffle is a uniform golden brown with a tender, crisp crust, a light and slightly moist inside and a pleasing flavor.

□ *What can I add to make waffles special?*

Sprinkle blueberries, whole bran cereal, cooked bacon pieces, granola or chopped nuts over batter immediately after pouring it onto iron before baking.

□ *Sometimes my waffles stick!*

Use a pastry brush to grease the waffle iron thoroughly, if necessary, between waffles. Or buy a waffle iron with nonstick grids.

# Breads, Yeast

Baking with yeast is perhaps the most satisfying of the culinary arts and far easier than you may think. Actively kneading and shaping the loaves and rolls is fun and relaxing, and you can use the time-consuming rising and baking periods for other tasks. Finally, your real reward is in the tender, golden-crusted bakings you take fresh and fragrant, from the oven.

## Yeast Loaves

A perfect loaf of bread is one of the highest achievements of a good cook. Whether you bake as an economy, for the pleasure it brings your family or as a hobby, breadmaking is a skill well worth learning. The greatest secret? Choose a reliable recipe, follow instructions exactly — and practice!

### Problems and Solutions

□ *What are the qualities of good bread?*

A good loaf of bread is symmetrical and has an evenly browned crust with a smooth, nicely rounded top. (Batter bread may have a pebbled surface.) It is slightly moist and soft with a tender crust, even texture (unkneaded batter breads may be coarser in texture), a fresh, tempting aroma and a wheatlike flavor.

□ *What is meant by "batter breads"?*

Batter breads are shortcut no-knead yeast breads. Ingredients are simply mixed, then the batter is spread in a pan to rise and bake.

□ *What is meant by sourdough bread?*

Sourdough, named for its unique flavor, won fame in gold rush days when each prospector carried his own pot of starter (a mixture of yeast, water and flour) for making breads and griddle cakes. Modern sourdough starters provide an adventure in old-time baking, but sourdough breads made at home cannot duplicate the special hard crust of a bakery sourdough loaf.

□ *Why is temperature so important to yeast?*

Yeast is sensitive to the right temperature (105° to 115°F). Too much heat will kill it, while cold will retard its action. Either way the bread won't rise.

□ *What are the ingredients in yeast breads and what do they do?*

**Flour** (mostly all-purpose enriched), which contains gluten, is the structure builder. When flour is mixed with liquid and kneaded or beaten, the proteins in it form gluten, which stretches like elastic, trapping bubbles of gas formed by the yeast to give bread its cellular structure. Because special-flavor flours (rye, whole wheat) develop fewer gluten strands, they most often are used in combination with all-purpose flour.

**Yeast** is a live plant which gives off a gas that makes dough rise. To perform well, yeast requires careful and precise measurements of water (at the right temperature) and other yeast bread ingredients.

**Sweeteners** such as sugar, honey or molasses provide food for the yeast, add flavor and help the crust of bread to brown.

**Salt** helps control yeast growth and prevents overrising, which can cause bread to collapse.

**Fat** is added for tenderness and flavor.

**Eggs** are sometimes added for taste, richness and color.

**Sour cream**, cheese, herbs and other flavorings can be added for variety in flavor.

*□ How do I make a perfect loaf of bread?*

**1. Check** water temperature with a thermometer. If it is 105° to 115°F, sprinkle on the granular yeast and stir until dissolved.

**2. After** the first addition of flour has been beaten in, the dough will be quite soft and will fall in "sheets" off the spoon.

**3. The second** addition of flour makes the dough stiff enough to knead. Add and mix in only enough so dough leaves side of bowl.

**4. To knead,** fold dough toward you. With heels of hands, push dough away with short rocking motions. Turn quarter turn; repeat.

**5. When** the dough is properly kneaded, it will feel elastic and the surface will appear smooth and blistered.

**6. Dough** should rise in a warm (80° to 85°F) draft-free place. You may put bowl of dough on wire rack over hot water and cover with towel

**7. Dough** should rise until double. Test by pressing fingertips ½ inch into dough. Impression will remain if dough has risen enough.

**8. Punch** center of dough down with your fist. Fold over and form into a ball. This releases large air bubbles to produce a finer texture.

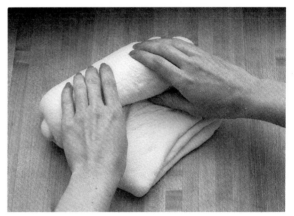

**9. To form** a regular loaf of bread, flatten dough into a rectangle, 18 × 9 inches. Fold crosswise into thirds, overlapping the two ends.

**10. Roll** dough tightly toward you, beginning at one of the open ends. Press to seal after each turn. Pinch roll firmly to seal.

**11. With** the side of your hand, press each end to seal; fold ends under. Place seam side down in a greased loaf pan to rise.

**12. Bake** loaves with tops of pans in the middle of the oven. To test for doneness, tap with wooden spoon: It will sound hollow.

## Problems and Solutions

□ *What happens if bread is kneaded for less time than the recipe states?*

If kneaded too little, bread will be coarse, heavy, crumbly and dry.

□ *Why do my bread loaves have lightly browned sides?*

Shiny bread pans do not cause bread to become brown as it bakes. Anodized aluminum, darkened metal or glass pans are best to produce well-browned crusts.

□ *Why does a big air pocket form under the top crust of my bread?*

This usually happens when dough is allowed to rise too long. (Refer to page 26 for how to test bread to determine the correct rising time.)

□ *My dough didn't rise!*

The yeast could have been too old; always check the package expiration date. It's wise to double-check the water temperature, too. And be sure to measure all ingredients accurately. Correct measurements are very important in baking with yeast. For example, too much salt retards the growth of the yeast and sometimes kills it.

□ *What should I do when my dough is too lively to roll out?*

When dough springs back again and again as you roll it, just cover it with a towel and allow it to rest 5 to 10 minutes. Dough will relax and roll out more easily.

□ *The sides of my otherwise beautiful loaves look slightly shredded.*

"Shred" is normal in a good loaf of baked bread. It is the result of the crust breaking on one or both sides of the loaf as it bakes. The shred can be fine or rough and looks as if the dough has been stretched.

□ *Why does my bread have a coarse texture?*

You may have let the dough or shaped loaves rise too long.

□ *Why did my loaves fall during baking?*

If the dough was allowed to rise too long before baking, the strands of gluten in the flour (refer to page 25) were stretched too far, causing the bread to collapse.

□ *Can I freeze dough before baking it?*

No, home freezers are not designed for the quick freezing required by unbaked dough to ensure satisfactory rising and baking.

□ *What is the difference in handling between yeast roll dough and bread dough?*

Dough for yeast rolls is richer and softer than bread dough, with more sugar and shortening plus eggs. Add the second amount of flour gradually, adding only enough so that dough can be handled without sticking.

□ *Can I knead my bread dough with an electric mixer?*

A standard counter-top mixer with dough hook attachment mixes the dough enough for satisfactory loaves of bread. The loaves may have slightly less volume than those kneaded by hand. A heavy-duty mixer yields loaves of higher volumes than does a standard counter-top mixer. Be sure to follow the manufacturer's directions for mixing time.

□ *My bread browns on top before the baking time is up.*

Cover the brown tops loosely with aluminum foil and continue baking for the required time.

# Yeast Rolls

Homemade yeast rolls are a luxury in today's busy life-styles. Fresh-from-the-oven sweet rolls — tender, soft and drizzled with icing, dolloped with fruit preserves and sometimes sprinkled with nuts — are the crowning touch for breakfast or coffee party. Served with dinner, your light and perfectly shaped, delicately golden rolls are company fare that can turn a simple family meal into a feast.

☐ *How do I shape rolls?*

## Problem and Solution

☐ *How do I refrigerate sweet roll dough?*

Mix the dough, grease the top well, cover with moistureproof wrap and a damp cloth; keep the cloth damp. Refrigerate up to three days if dough contains ¼ cup sugar or more. When ready to bake, cut off as much dough as you need and shape into rolls; let rise until double and a fingertip indentation remains (1½ to 2 hours). Bake as directed in recipe.

**Cloverleaf Rolls:** Shape dough into smooth 1-inch balls; place 3 balls in each greased muffin cup. Brush with softened margarine. Let rise and bake.

**Casseroles:** Shape dough into 1-inch balls; place in greased round pan. Brush with softened margarine or butter. Let rise and bake.

**Pan Biscuits:** Roll yeast dough on well-floured surface into rectangle about ⅜-inch thick; gently lift and place in greased rectangular pan. Cut dough into rectangles and brush with softened margarine or butter. Let rise and bake.

**Crescent Rolls:** Roll dough about ¼-inch thick into 12-inch circle. Spread with softened margarine. Cut into 16 wedges; roll up tightly. Place rolls, with points underneath, on greased cookie sheet; curve slightly. Brush with margarine. Let rise and bake.

# Cakes & Frostings

Cakes play an important role at many significant occasions in our lives. Whether they depend largely on eggs for a batter as airy as sea-foam, are jam-packed with nuts and fruit for the holidays or are tender and rich because of the proportion of shortening in them, cakes — often crowned with luscious frostings — are as American as apple pie and just as easy to make.

## Foam-Type Cakes

**Angel food** cakes are made without leavening, egg yolks or shortening and contain a very high proportion of beaten egg whites to flour.

**Sponge** cakes depend on separately beaten egg yolks and whites, and leavening for lightness, but contain no shortening.

**Chiffon** cakes, like angel food cakes, depend on beaten egg whites and sugar (meringue) for lightness; like sponge cakes, they contain egg yolks and leavening and in addition, oil for shortening.

### Problems and Solutions

☐ *Why shouldn't the tube pan be greased for angel food, chiffon and sponge cakes?*

The pan must be ungreased so that the delicate batter can cling to the sides of the pan for support as it bakes and cools.

☐ *How should I store a foam-type cake baked one day to serve the next?*

A foam-type cake will stay fresh overnight stored in the pan and covered with waxed paper. Remove it from the pan and frost it the day you serve it.

☐ *My angel food cake had large holes and was gummy and low in volume.*

Underbeating the egg whites could cause coarse, low-volume cakes.

☐ *My angelfood cake was high in volume but was coarse in texture.*

Underfolding can cause a coarse texture in an otherwise beautiful, high cake.

☐ *When are the beaten egg whites for my angel food or chiffon cake stiff enough?*

To test, cut a rubber spatula through the egg whites. It should leave a definite path, and when lifted, the beaten egg whites on the spatula should stand in stiff, straight peaks.

☐ *I never know what is meant by "fold" in angel food cake recipes.*

To fold (or incorporate the flour-sugar mixture gradually into the beaten egg white mixture), cut down through the center of the beaten egg whites, along bottom and up the sides. Rotate bowl ¼ turn; repeat. Follow the recipe for the degree of folding indicated, such as "just until flour-sugar mixture disappears" or "just until blended."

□ *Why does chiffon cake have a rubbery layer on the bottom.*

A layer on the bottom of a chiffon cake is caused by underbeating the egg white mixture or by too much folding, which breaks down the egg white mixture that supports the batter.

□ *There are big holes in the sides and bottom of my angel food cake.*

Those holes are air pockets where the stiff batter did not touch the pan. To avoid air pockets, run a knife in a spiral pattern through the batter in the tube pan, pushing it gently against the tube.

□ *My angel food cake was compact and tough.*

Overbeating or overfolding could break down the egg whites and result in a compact cake.

□ *My angel food cake pulled away from the sides of the pan and fell out as it was cooling.*

A cake that pulls away and/or falls out of the pan is underbaked. Check your oven (refer to page 134) to be sure it is not baking at too low a temperature. Test the cake for doneness by touching the cracks. If they are dry, the cake is done.

# Fruitcake

Who can imagine the holidays without colorful fruitcake? Often made from a cherished family recipe, these sumptuous cakes are more fruit than batter — so rich that a sliver of a slice can satisfy.

## Problems and Solutions

□ *Why should fruitcake pans be lined with greased aluminum foil?*

Fruitcake pans are lined with greased foil for easy removal of the cakes and to prevent overbrowning during baking.

□ *How can I thinly slice fruitcake so it doesn't crumble?*

For easiest slicing and a mellow flavor, fruitcake should be made three to four weeks ahead of time, then wrapped and stored in the refrigerator. If you like, drizzle cakes with wine or brandy before wrapping or wrap in wine-dampened cloth and place in tightly covered container in refrigerator. Cut fruitcake with a thin, nonserrated or electric knife.

# Shortening-Type Cakes

All shortening-type cakes contain essentially the same ingredients — only the flavors differ. So choose tested recipes and follow them carefully. It's easy to win admiration for beautiful cakes that strike a festive note on any occasion.

## Problems and Solutions

☐ *What are the characteristics of a good shortening-type cake?*

A good shortening-type cake is light and has a slightly rounded, smooth, tender top. It is fine-grained with an even texture (not crumbly), is light, tender, soft, velvety, slightly moist and has a pleasant, sweet flavor.

☐ *Should cakes be baked in shiny pans?*

Yes. Shiny pans which reflect heat instead of absorbing it are necessary to produce cakes with delicate, tender crusts.

☐ *Why do my cakes stick to the pans?*

Too little greasing or leaving cakes in the pans too long can cause sticking. Grease the pans generously (1 tablespoon shortening for each layer pan), using a pastry brush to get in the corners. Remove the layers from the pans after cooling about 5 minutes.

☐ *I added raisins to my cake and they all fell to the bottom!*

Because cakes with thinner batters cannot hold larger pieces of fruits and/or nuts in suspension, they fall to the bottom. Add fruit and nuts only when included in the recipe, or chop them very fine.

☐ *Can I make a cake and freeze it to serve another time?*

Yes, but cakes freeze best unfrosted. Frosted cakes can be frozen, but it is nice to remember that creamy frostings freeze better than fluffy or whipped cream frostings.

To prevent frosting from sticking to wrapping, freeze cake 1 hour, insert wooden picks around the top and side of cake, and wrap.

☐ *My cake had large holes in it.*

Too much shortening and insufficient beating can cause coarse texture. Again, be sure you follow the recipe exactly and use accurate measuring equipment.

☐ *I have some cake molds (a lamb and a heart). How full should I fill them with batter before baking?*

Never fill a mold more than ½ full.

# Frostings

Like grandmother's famous powdered sugar and white mountain frostings, today's frostings are a cake's crowning glory. The skills are well worth learning because what's a cake without its frosting?

## Problems and Solutions

☐ *I'm a beginning baker, but I want to make attractive cupcakes. Have you any tips?*

**Make a spiral design** (1) on top of a frosted cupcake by placing tip of metal spatula lightly at outer edge and drawing spatula slowly toward center as you turn the cupcake.

**Decorate** (2) the top of a cupcake with dainty scallop designs by frosting with creamy frosting, then pressing the tip of an inverted teaspoon lightly into the frosting in even rows.

**Scatter** (3) crushed peppermint candy, chopped nuts or candy sprinkles around the edge of a frosted cupcake for a border.

**Spell out** (4) a message with miniature chocolate chips or cinnamon candies on a cupcake that has been frosted with creamy frosting.

☐ *What are the qualities of a good frosting?*

A good frosting has a soft, lustrous appearance and a smooth consistency that holds swirls. It is soft enough to spread but remains on the cake without running down the side.

☐ *Why did my fluffy frosting sink into the cake the day after I frosted it?*

Because so much air is incorporated into fluffy frostings, they are not as stable as creamy frostings. It's best to serve a cake with fluffy frosting on the day it is made. If you must store the cake overnight, place it under a cake safe or an inverted bowl, but slip a knife blade under the rim so the cover is not airtight.

☐ *Why does my creamy frosting pull and tear the cake when I try to spread it?*

Your frosting is probably too thick to spread on a delicate cake. Try thinning a small amount of frosting with a few drops of water or milk, then coating the side of the cake with a thin layer as shown below, to seal in crumbs. Swirl remaining frosting over the cake, using a small flexible spatula, and frost cake with a "light" touch to avoid tearing. If frosting is still too thick, add a little liquid.

☐ *How can I keep paper liners from falling off my cupcakes?*

Fill the cupcake liners about ⅔ full, then frost baked, cooled cupcakes to the very edge, sealing the frostings to the liners.

☐ *Can I store cakes with creamy frostings?*

Yes, these cakes are best stored under a cake safe or covered loosely with aluminum foil. If the cake has a pudding filling, refrigerate at once for no longer than 2 days.

☐ *How do I frost a 2-layer cake?*

**Lay** 4 strips of waxed paper around edge of cake plate. Brush away any loose crumbs. Place a cooled cake layer on plate, rounded side down. (The waxed paper will protect plate as you frost and can be removed later.)

**Spread** about ½ cup of creamy frosting (⅓ cup if fluffy frosting) over the top of first layer to within about ¼ inch of the edge.

**Place** the second layer, rounded side up, on the first layer so that the 2 flat sides of the layers are together with frosting in between. Coat the side of the cake with a very thin layer of frosting to seal in the crumbs.

**Frost** the side of the cake in swirls, making a rim about ¼ inch high above the top of the cake to prevent top from appearing sloped. Spread remaining frosting on top, just to the built-up rim.

# Decorators' Frosting

## Problems and Solutions

☐ *What are the characteristics of a good decorators' frosting?*

A good decorators' frosting is soft enough to flow through a decorators' tube, yet firm enough to hold its shape on the cake. The color is harmonious with the other colors used to decorate the cake.

☐ *I have received a cake decorating kit as a gift. How do I learn to use it?*

Read the directions carefully for assembly and use. Make some decorators' frosting and practice the techniques described on an inverted cake pan.

☐ *Air bubbles spurt out of the frosting tip when I use it.*

To prevent air bubbles, pack the frosting to the end of the tube, then squeeze out a little frosting to expel any air before you begin to decorate.

☐ *Sometimes the tip of my decorating cone gets blocked with frosting.*

Open the tip with a pin or remove tip and wash it.

☐ *I have no decorating tips or bag. What can I use instead to decorate my cake?*

You can make a cone from a paper envelope. Place about ⅓ cup of frosting in the corner of an envelope. Fold the sides toward the center. Snip off a small corner to make a tip.

☐ *How do you use a decorating cone?*

**Fold** back about 4 inches of the top of the decorating bag (this keeps the edges of the bag clean when the frosting is added).

**Fit** the tip tightly into the cone with one finger.

**Fill** bag only about ½ full with decorating frosting for easy handling.

**Fold** the top of the bag down to keep the frosting in place.

**Hold** the cone with one hand near the top to keep the cone closed. Use the other hand to guide the tip.

**Make** most designs by holding the cone at a 45° angle; for drop flowers and rosettes, hold the cone vertically. Using steady pressure, press out the frosting, twist the cone and lift point up and away.

# Candy

With "store-bought" candy fast becoming a luxury item and homemade gifts more prized now than ever before, it will pay you to learn a few basic success secrets for your own "candy kitchen" at home.

## Problems and Solutions

☐ *Can I double the recipe when making penuche or other candy?*

No, make one recipe of candy at a time. Doubling a recipe will change the cooking time and affect the quality of the candy.

☐ *Why should I use a candy thermometer?*

A candy thermometer should be used to gauge exact cooking temperatures. When using a thermometer, stand it upright in the cooking mixture; the bulb should not rest on the bottom of the pan. Read the thermometer at eye level and watch closely as the temperature rises.

☐ *Why does the same candy, cooked the same way, vary from day to day?*

A cool, dry atmosphere is best for candy making because heat, humidity and altitude can affect results adversely. On a rainy day, candy should be cooked to a temperature a degree or so higher than the recipe indicates.

☐ *What makes my candy crystallize or become grainy instead of creamy?*

Even a single grain of sugar can start crystallization. It is important to dissolve the sugar completely over low heat and to remove any sugar grains from the side of the pan.

Cover pan briefly after the sugar has dissolved so that any remaining grains of sugar will be washed down into the cooking mixture.

Do not stir the syrup after it boils and has become completely clear. Stirring the syrup or scraping the pan during cooling also produces crystals and should be avoided.

☐ *I don't own a candy thermometer. How do I test candy without it?*

Candy can also be tested by the cold water method. Using a clean spoon, drop a small amount of cooking mixture into a cupful of very cold water to cool it quickly. Test the hardness with your fingers. If mixture is too soft for the type of candy (below), return pan to heat and continue cooking.

## Candy Cooking Tests

| Stage of Hardness | Temperature | Cold Water Test |
|---|---|---|
| Thread | 223°-234°F (106°-112°C) | Forms a 2-inch soft thread |
| Soft ball | 234°-240°F (112°-116°C) | Forms a ball but does not hold its shape |
| Firm ball | 242°-248°F (117°-120°C) | Forms a ball that holds its shape until pressed |
| Hard ball | 250°-268°F (121°-131°C) | Forms a ball that holds its shape but is pliable |
| Soft crack | 270°-290°F (132°-143°C) | Separates into hard but not brittle threads |
| Hard crack | 300°-310°F (149°-154°C) | Separates into hard and brittle threads |
| Caramel | 320°-350°F (160°-177°C) | Coats a spoon and forms a light caramel-colored molten mass when poured onto a plate (do not drop into cold water) |

# Chocolate Flavoring

Why does chocolate turn "white"? How can I make chocolate curls? These are some of the questions asked often by lovers of that universally popular flavoring, chocolate. You'll find the answers below and other chocolate information on page 132.

**Chocolate** results from grinding roasted and shelled cocoa beans. It ranges from bitter to sweet in flavor.

**Cocoa** powder is a term for the solid substance that remains after a portion of the cocoa butter has been removed from chocolate. Carob powder, from the pod of the carob bean, is milder than cocoa and sweeter than chocolate and is sometimes used as a cocoa substitute in cakes, candy, ice cream and puddings.

## Problems and Solutions

☐ *Why does chocolate harden as it melts?*

Chocolate may harden or tighten during melting if there is only the smallest amount of water or steam in the melting pan. If chocolate tightens, it can be returned to creamy consistency by stirring in about 1 teaspoon solid vegetable shortening for each ounce of chocolate being melted.

☐ *Why does chocolate "whiten" in storage?*

The white color or "bloom" on chocolate occurs when a rise in temperature of only a few degrees causes the cocoa butter to melt and rise to the surface of the chocolate. As the chocolate cools, the cocoa butter turns a misty grey color. Bloom does not affect the flavor of the chocolate and will disappear during melting. The ideal storage temperature for chocolate is 78°F.

☐ *How can I substitute cocoa for unsweetened chocolate?*

In emergencies, 3 tablespoons unsweetened cocoa plus 1 tablespoon vegetable shortening can be substituted for 1 ounce unsweetened chocolate in some recipes.

☐ *How do I melt chocolate?*

Chocolate can be melted in a heavy saucepan over low heat when combined with liquid or fat. When melting the chocolate alone, avoid scorching the chocolate by melting it in a small, heatproof bowl in hot water or in the top of a double boiler over hot (not boiling) water. Two chocolate squares at a time also can be melted in the microwave uncovered on medium (50%) 3 to 4 minutes, stirring after 2½ minutes. Chocolate chips (½ to 1 cup) can be microwaved uncovered on medium (50%) 3 to 4½ minutes. Because they retain their shape as they soften, chocolate chips should be stirred until smooth. Avoid overcooking.

☐ *How do I make chocolate curls?*

Shave chocolate or make curls with a swivel-bladed vegetable parer or thin, sharp knife by slicing across a block of sweet milk chocolate in long, thin strokes. The curls will be easier to make if the chocolate is slightly warm. Let chocolate stand in a warm place for about 15 minutes before slicing. Curls will be slightly smaller if made with semisweet chocolate. Lift curls with a wooden pick to avoid breakage.

# Condiments

Pungent, spicy, tangy flavors — some like more, others less. Relishes, sauces, mustards and vinegars served at the table let everyone season food to personal taste. Choose from hundreds of condiments at the market; make some special ones at home.

## Catsup

Catsup, catchup or ketchup is prepared from concentrated tomato pulp, vinegar, onion, spices and sweeteners. Catsup also can be made with mushrooms or green tomatoes. It is used as a table condiment on meat, potatoes and eggs.

## Chutney

Chutney is a relish made of mixed fruits or vegetables and used to accompany meats.

**Apple** chutney is sweet, thick and spicy and is served with pork.

**Cranberry** chutney is a combination of cranberries, raisins, vinegar and spices and is served with poultry or over cream cheese as an appetizer.

**Mango** chutney can be hot or mild and is served with Indian foods flavored with curry.

**Tomato** chutney can be sweet or spicy, red or green and is served with vegetables.

## Horseradish

Horseradish is grown for its taproot, which is grated and mixed with oil, powdered milk, vinegar and salt. It can be mixed with mayonnaise to make a sauce. Horseradish is served with meat, poultry and egg dishes.

## Mustards

**American** (1) mustard is mild, sweet and pale yellow in color and has the consistency of a thick sauce. It is often added with mayonnaise to egg, fish and potato salads and is an accompaniment to frankfurters and hamburgers.

**Chinese** mustard is very hot and light yellow in color and is made from dry mustard and water or vinegar. As a dipping sauce, it adds zest to egg rolls and other Oriental foods.

**English** mustard is hot and deep yellow in color, has a coarse texture and is made from ground rather than pounded mustard seeds. In England, this hot mustard is served with roast beef, chops and steaks as well as with cheese dishes and meat pies.

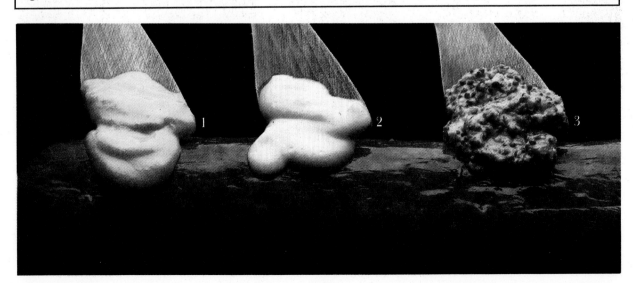

**French** (2) mustard comes in several varieties and is strong but more subtle in flavor than English mustard. Dijon-style mustard, creamy grey-yellow in color, originated in France and also is made in several varieties of different strengths according to standards and regulations determined hundreds of years ago. Dijon-style mustards, also made in the United States, are popular in cooking for enhancing the flavor of foods and sauces.

**German** (3) mustards range from mild, coarse-grained and pale yellow in color to strong, extra hot and brown in color. The milder mustards are served with bland sausages made of veal, the stronger mustards with highly seasoned sausages like knockwurst.

# Vinegars

Vinegars come in many varieties, strengths, colors and flavors.

**Cider** (1) vinegar is made from the juice of apples by a natural process of alcoholic and acetous fermentation. It is amber in color and used for cooking and in salad dressings. Vinegar used for pickling should be 5 to 6 percent acidity. Cider vinegar is also used in chutneys and vinaigrette dressings.

**Distilled** vinegar is colorless and strong in flavor. It is used for pickling foods such as cocktail onions in which lack of color is desirable.

**Flavored** vinegar is wine vinegar flavored with fruit — raspberries or strawberries (2); herbs — basil, tarragon (3) or mint; shallots or garlic. Flavored vinegar can be made by adding fresh herbs to a bottle of wine vinegar. Cover and let stand at room temperature for a week before straining vinegar.

**Malt** vinegar, made from barley malt or cereals, has a strong flavor and a caramel color. It is used in pickling and traditionally accompanies English fish and chips.

**Rice** vinegar is sweet and delicate in flavor and used in Oriental cooking. Its color, which can be white, red or black, determines the foods with which it is cooked.

**Spirit** vinegar is strong and colorless. It is sometimes flavored with lemon and is used in pickling and sauces.

**Wine** (4) vinegar is strong, aromatic and red or white in color. It is made from red, white or rosé wine or sherry. Its color determines its use for mayonnaise, vinaigrette salad dressings and marinades.

# Cookies

The aroma of fresh-baked cookies drifting from your kitchen on a cold or rainy afternoon says "welcome home" in the warmest way. Served as a snack or a quick dessert or sent to a friend through the mail, cookies are a wholesome way to express a caring thought. There are basically six kinds of cookies; bar, drop, molded, pressed, refrigerated and rolled. Bar and drop cookies are easiest to make. If you have problems with your cookie baking, we suggest the following how-to tips.

## Problems and Solutions

☐ *What kind of cookie sheet should I use for best baking results?*

A shiny, bright cookie sheet at least 2 inches narrower and shorter than the oven is best for evenly browned cookies. The sheet may be open on one, two or three sides. If a coated cookie sheet is used, watch carefully for browning.

☐ *Can whole wheat flour be substituted for all-purpose flour in cookies?*

Yes, many cookies can be made with a direct substitution of whole wheat flour, although it is best to use recipes tested with whole wheat flour. Drop, molded, pressed or refrigerator cookie dough with the full-bodied flavor of stone-ground whole wheat flour may spread more in baking, and cookies may have a coarser texture than cookies made with all-purpose flour.

☐ *Where should I place cookie sheets in the oven during baking?*

For delicately browned cookies, place one cookie sheet at a time on the center oven rack.

☐ *How should I store cookies?*

Store *crisp, thin cookies* in a loosely covered container in a dry climate, tightly covered container in damp, humid climate. Store *soft, unfrosted cookies* in a tightly covered container to preserve their moisture. Store *frosted cookies* in a single layer in a covered container so that frosting will maintain its shape and the cookies will retain their moistness.

☐ *How should I wrap cookies for mailing?*

**Choose** cookies such as drop cookies or bake bar cookies in a disposable foil pan that can be mailed. These cookies are less fragile and travel better than thin, crisp cookies.

**Wrap** cookies separately or back to back in pairs in plastic wrap, aluminum foil, waxed paper or small plastic bags.

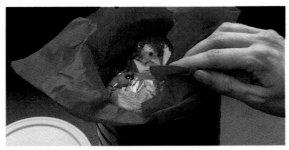

**Pack** wrapped cookies in a coffee can or sturdy box, filling the container as full as practical and padding the top with crushed paper to prevent shaking or breakage. Pack containers in a foil-lined corrugated or fiberboard packing box. For filler, use crumpled newspaper or shredded paper.

**Seal** packing box with tape; wrap tightly in heavy paper. Address in large print directly on package or on a gummed mailing label. Cover address with transparent tape to protect it from becoming blurred.

# Bar Cookies

**Problems and Solutions**

☐ *What are some of the qualities of good bar cookies?*

Bar cookies cut well, are rich, moist and flavorful and do not have dry edges.

☐ *How can I prevent my bar cookies from crumbling when cut?*

Bar cookies are less crumbly and easier to cut if cooled in the pan before cutting.

☐ *What causes my bar cookies to be hard and crusty after baking?*

Overbaking causes hard and crusty bar cookies. The correct size of pan is important, too. If the pan is larger than recommended, the dough will be thin and bars will become hard from overbaking.

☐ *What causes my bar cookies to be soft and doughy in the center?*

Underbaking causes doughy bar cookies. If the pan is smaller than recommended, dough will be thick and will not bake completely in the time indicated in recipe. Test bars for doneness before removing from oven.

# Drop Cookies

**Problems and Solutions**

☐ *How can I decorate my drop cookies before baking?*

Press candied fruit or nuts into the mounds of cookie dough before baking.

☐ *What are some of the qualities of a good drop cookie?*

A good drop cookie is uniform in size and shape, delicate, brown, tender and rich.

☐ *Why do my cookies bake together?*

Because cookies spread while baking, drop spoonfuls of dough about 2 inches apart. Chill soft dough before dropping onto cookie sheet to prevent excessive spreading during baking. Let cookie sheet cool between bakings.

☐ *Why are my drop cookies too brown on the bottoms but not the top?*

Dark-colored or coated cookie sheets or cookie sheets that are too large for the size of the oven cause excessive browning on the bottoms of cookies. See question on kind of cookie sheet on page 40. Overbaking or too hot an oven also results in dark bottoms and dry, hard cookies.

# Molded Cookies

## Problems and Solutions

☐ *What are some of the qualities of a good molded cookie?*

A good molded cookie is uniform in shape, delicately browned, crisp and tender.

☐ *What can I do if my cookie dough is too soft to mold?*

If your dough is still soft after chilling, mix in 1 to 2 tablespoons flour.

☐ *What can I do if my dough is too dry and crumbly to mold?*

Work 1 to 2 tablespoons water, cream, milk or softened butter into dough with your hands.

# Pressed Cookies

## Problems and Solutions

☐ *What are some of the qualities of a good pressed cookie?*

A good pressed cookie is uniform in pattern and shape, tender and crisp with a rich, buttery flavor.

☐ *Why is it so hard to force dough through my cookie press?*

If the dough is too stiff or too cold, it will be hard to press into shapes. Test the dough for consistency before adding all the flour. To do this, put a small amount of dough in the cookie press and squeeze out. The dough should be soft and pliable but not crumbly. If dough is too stiff, add 1 egg yolk.

☐ *Why doesn't cookie dough holds its shape when forced through my cookie press?*

Dough that is too soft will lose its shape when pressed. Add 1 to 2 tablespoons flour to make the dough firmer.

☐ *How can I prevent pressed cookie dough from spreading and losing its shape during baking?*

Be sure your cookie sheet is cool before pressing out cookie dough. A hot cookie sheet causes cookie dough to soften and spread before baking. Follow recipe exactly; don't over-measure shortening.

# Refrigerator Cookies

## Problems and Solutions

☐ *What are some of the qualities of a good refrigerator cookie?*

A good refrigerator cookie is uniform in shape, thin, rich, crisp and light brown in color unless flavored with chocolate or molasses.

☐ *How to I shape cookie dough into rolls before refrigerating?*

Shape dough with hands into long, smooth rolls of the diameter recipe suggests. If desired, add a decorative touch by rolling in finely chopped nuts, colored sugar or chocolate shot. Wrap in waxed paper, twisting ends. Chill in refrigerator or freezer until firm enough to slice easily.

☐ *Can I keep refrigerated dough if I don't bake it all at one time?*

Yes, rolls of dough can be refrigerated wrapped for several weeks or frozen in moistureproof, vaporproof wrapping as long as 12 months.

☐ *Why are my refrigerated cookies soft instead of crisp?*

Cutting the chilled dough too thick or under-baking results in soft cookies.

# Rolled Cookies

## Problems and Solutions

☐ *What are some of the qualities of a good rolled cookie?*

A good rolled cookie retains the shape of the cutter, is light brown on edge and bottom unless chocolate or molasses, and is crisp and tender to bite.

☐ *How can I keep dough from sticking to the board and rolling pin?*

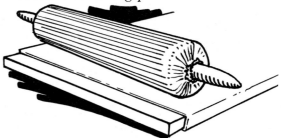

Use a pastry cloth and a stockinet-covered rolling pin to make rolling of dough easier and help prevent dough from sticking. Rub flour evenly into rolling pin cover and pastry cloth for easy handling. Roll dough lightly and evenly before cutting cookies.

☐ *How can I prevent my rolled cookies from becoming dry and tough?*

Too much flour and rerolling the dough results in dry, tough cookies. Use only enough flour to prevent the dough from sticking during rolling. Cut cookie shapes close together, leaving as little dough as possible to reroll.

# Dairy Foods

On pasta and casseroles, in salads and toasted sandwiches, with bread and fruit or a glass of wine, cheese can fill a hundred chinks in your meal plans with satisfying nourishment. And like cream, milk and yogurt in cooking, cheese enriches every dish it touches. For more about cheeses, see the chart opposite.

## Cheese

Cheeses of all flavors and textures can be divided into two categories — natural cheese and cheese blends.

**Natural** cheese is made from the milk or cream of cows, sheep or goats and is usually cured or aged to develop flavor.

**Cheese blends** are mixtures of one or more cheeses and additions such as water, milk solids, spices, flavorings and other ingredients. Softer than natural cheeses, they can be melted, blended with other foods or spread easily on bread or crackers.

### Problems and Solutions

☐ *At what temperature should I serve natural cheese?*

For full flavor and best texture, serve most cheeses at room temperature. Remove cheese from refrigerator 30 to 60 minutes before serving. Exceptions are cottage, cream and Neufchâtel, which are soft, unripened cheeses and should be served chilled, Naturally soft, refined cheeses, such as Camembert and Liederkranz, should be removed from the refrigerator several hours before serving for best flavor.

☐ *How do I shred a small amount of cheese?*

Pull a swivel-bladed vegetable parer over the edge of firm cheese to shred a small amount.

☐ *How much cheese should I buy when a recipe calls for 1 cup?*

Four ounces of natural or process cheese equal 1 cup of shredded or cubed cheese.

☐ *How do I cut Bleu or Roquefort cheese without it crumbling?*

Mold-ripened cheeses can be cut easily and cleanly with dental floss or heavy thread.

☐ *How do I freeze and thaw firm cheeses?*

Freeze cheese in small amounts in tightly wrapped packages up to 4 months. Thaw cheese in refrigerator to prevent crumbling. Save leftover cheese bits to blend with cream for spreads and dips.

☐ *How can I prevent cooked cheese from becoming stringy?*

Cook at low temperature and avoid overcooking to prevent cheese from becoming stringy. Add cheese in small pieces or shreds to casseroles and sauces for even, quick melting. Cream and Neufchâtel cheeses blend easily when first softened at room temperature.

☐ *How do I shred soft cheese?*

Very soft cheese shreds more easily if first placed in the freezer for fifteen minutes. Or it can be finely chopped instead of shredded.

## Varieties of Natural Cheeses

| Texture | Flavor | Use |
| --- | --- | --- |
| **Hard** | | |
| Kashkaval | salty | appetizer, dessert |
| Parmesan | piquant, sharp | cooking, salad, seasoning |
| Provolone | mild to sharp, smoky | cooking, pasta |
| Romano | piquant, sharp | cooking, pasta, seasoning |
| Swiss | mild, nutty, sweet | appetizer, cooking, dessert, sandwich |
| **Firm** | | |
| Bleu | tangy, sharp, robust | appetizer, dessert, salad |
| Cheddar | mild to very sharp | cooking, dessert, with fruit |
| Cheshire | rich, robust | cooking, with fruit |
| Edam, Gouda | milky, nutty | appetizer, dessert |
| Fontina | mellow, mild | appetizer, dessert, eggs |
| Gjetost | caramel, sweet | sandwich, snack |
| Gorgonzola | piquant, salty | dessert, salad |
| Gruyère | nutty, slightly sharp | cooking, dessert |
| **Semisoft** | | |
| Bel Paese | creamy, mild | cooking, dessert |
| Brick | mild to sharp | appetizer, sandwich |
| Feta | salty, sharp | cooking, salad |
| Monterey Jack | creamy, mild | appetizer, cooking, sandwich |
| Mozzarella | mild | cooking, pizza |
| Muenster | mild to sharp | appetizer, dessert, sandwich |
| Port du Salut | mild to robust | appetizer, dessert, sandwich |
| Roquefort | salty, sharp | appetizer, dessert, salad |
| Stilton | piquant, rich | dessert, salad, snack |
| **Soft** | | |
| Brie | mild to pungent | appetizer, dessert |
| Camembert | mild to pungent | appetizer, dessert, sandwich |
| Cottage, dry or creamed | mild | cooking, salad |
| Cream | very mild | appetizer, dessert, salad |
| Liederkranz | pungent | appetizer, dessert |
| Neufchâtel | mild | appetizer, dessert, salad, spread |
| Ricotta | mild | cooking, dessert, pasta stuffing |

# Cream

## Problems and Solutions

☐ *How do I store whipped cream?*

Store whipped cream in the refrigerator one to two hours; for longer storage, freeze dollops of whipped cream on aluminum foil. When frozen solid, wrap and store in freezer. Serve for dessert toppings or Irish coffee.

☐ *How do I whip cream?*

Chill bowl and beaters before whipping chilled cream; whip only until stiff. Overbeating or beating on low speed instead of high can cause cream to separate into fat and liquid.

☐ *How much does cream increase in volume after whipping?*

The whipping of cream causes it to approximately double in volume, depending on the fat content and temperature of the cream and the kind of beater used for whipping.

☐ *How much sugar should I add to sweeten whipped cream?*

Add 1 tablespoon granulated or powdered sugar for every ½ cup of chilled cream.

# Milk

## Problems and Solutions

☐ *What are the advantages of ultra heat treated milk?*

Ultra heat treated milk in aseptic paper packaging enables you to store quarts of milk without refrigeration for up to six months. Once opened, the milk needs refrigeration. Flavored milk is also aseptically packaged for shelf storage.

☐ *Can I substitute evaporated for sweetened condensed milk?*

No, evaporated and sweetened are not interchangeable because of the added sugar in sweetened condensed milk.

# Sour Cream

Sour cream is sweet cream that has been soured by the addition of lactic acid culture and has a milk-fat content of 18 to 20 percent.

## Problems and Solutions

☐ *How do I prevent sour cream from curdling during cooking?*

Overheating and overstirring can cause sour cream to become thin and curdle. To prevent this, add sour cream to flour or a condensed soup when making sauces or gravies or add to cooked mixtures just before serving time.

☐ *Can I freeze sour cream?*

Dairy sour cream should be stored in the refrigerator, never frozen. Some prepared foods made with sour cream, such as cookies and coffee cake, can be frozen.

# Yogurt

Yogurt is whole or partly skimmed milk fermented with a bacterial culture and has fewer calories than sour cream. Fruit or flavorings may be added to plain yogurt.

## Problem and Solution

☐ *How do I use yogurt in recipes?*

Fold or stir yogurt into other ingredients in recipe; avoid beating or overcooking, which destroys the creamy texture. Yogurt is found in many recipes for coffee cakes, quiches, refrigerated cream pies, stroganoff and other dishes. Yogurt can be combined with other ingredients for beverages and dressings and liquefied in the blender.

# Desserts

A dessert can be simple as pudding, rich as cheesecake, sophisticated as crepes suzette. Here are some all-time favorites with secrets for their success.

**Blintzes and crepes** are thin, light pancakes with fillings of cottage cheese, fruit or jam. Blintzes are browned on one side only, then filled, folded and cooked in margarine or butter and oil until golden brown. They are served warm with a topping or filling. Dessert crepes become crepes suzette when folded into triangles and flamed with orange-flavored liqueur.

## Problem and Solution

☐ *Can I make crepes ahead of time?*

Yes, crepes can be made ahead of time, layered between sheets of waxed paper and wrapped for future use. Crepes can be refrigerated for several days or stored in the freezer up to 3 months. Thaw, wrapped, at room temperature about 3 hours; fill and reheat in sauce in the oven or microwave.

**Cheesecakes** are rich, creamy, custardlike cakes made from a combination of cheese, eggs, cream, sugar and flavorings. They can be baked in a pastry, graham cracker or cookie crumb crust or made with gelatin and refrigerated and often are topped with sour cream or fruit.

## Problem and Solution

☐ *Can you please tell me how I can prevent my cheese cake from shrinking?*

Cheesecakes should be baked at a low temperature to prevent excess shrinkage. Refrigerate baked cheesecakes for at least 3 hours before serving, and be sure to refrigerate leftover portions immediately.

**Cobblers and pudding cakes** are baked in casseroles or baking dishes. Cobblers, similar to deep-dish pies, have a fruit base topped with a rich biscuit or pastry crust. Pudding cakes form a cake or biscuit topping over chocolate or lemon sauce during baking.

**Custards, pots de crème, puddings and dessert fondues** are sweet, creamy baked mixtures or smooth sauces cooked over boiling water or low heat. Hearty steamed puddings are similar to festive fruitcakes but are cooked in a steamer instead of baked. They are sliced and served warm with a sauce.

## Problem and Solution

☐ *When is baked custard done?*

Insert a knife halfway between center and edge of custard; if it comes out clean, the custard is done. The center of the custard may look soft but will become firm as it cools.

**Cream puffs and éclairs** are hollow, golden-brown pastry shells made from dough known as pâté à choux (cream puff pastry). Mounds of dough are baked until puffed and golden, like popovers, but all are symmetrical in shape with a more tender crust and thin, tender, crisp filaments inside. The puffs are cooled, slit and filled with whipped cream or custard just before serving.

## Problems and Solutions

☐ *Why don't my cream puffs puff up?*

Too much or too little water or too much or too little fat can prevent cream puff dough from rising. Follow the recipe exactly; use correct measuring equipment and methods.

□ *Can cream puffs be made ahead of time?*

Shaped cream puff dough (in puffs) can be frozen for no longer than 1 month. Bake frozen puffs at 400°F for 45 to 50 minutes. Baked puffs can be frozen up to 3 months. Thaw unwrapped at room temperature about 30 minutes.

□ *How can I improvise a steamer for my steamed puddings?*

A steamer can be improvised from a Dutch oven or large saucepan with a tight-fitting cover. Place a wire rack or trivet inside to raise the pudding about 1 inch above the bottom of the pan. Pudding molds can be heatproof ceramic or metal bowls, gelatin molds, custard cups or coffee cans as well as the traditional Turk's-head mold. Follow specific recipe for amount of water to add for steaming.

□ *Can I make steamed pudding ahead of time and reheat later?*

Yes, steamed puddings can be made ahead of time, wrapped and refrigerated or frozen. They can be reheated in the oven or microwave to serve warm. Timing in the microwave depends on the size of the pudding.

**Frozen** desserts can be made in many flavor variations of ice cream, sherbet and ices.

**Problems and Solutions**

□ *What are sorbets?*

Sorbets (the French word for sherbets), are partially frozen, sweetened fruit juices served between dinner courses or as dessert.

□ *How do I prevent the formation of ice crystals on ice cream?*

After scooping ice cream from a container, press a piece of plastic wrap or aluminum foil against the surface of the remaining ice cream to prevent ice crystals from forming. All frozen desserts should be stored in tightly closed containers at 0°F or lower.

□ *How can I scoop or cut ice cream easily?*

Soften very hard ice cream in the refrigerator for 10 to 20 minutes to make dipping or slicing easier. Use an electric knife to cut blocks of ice cream into smooth slices.

**Gelatin** desserts in a variety of textures and shapes can be made several hours or a day before serving.

## Problems and Solutions

☐ *Sometimes my unflavored gelatin doesn't jell; what am I doing wrong?*

Gelatin must be completely dissolved to jell. To dissolve, it should be mixed with the sugar in the recipe or sprinkled over cold liquid and stirred gently with a rubber spatula until all granules are separated. Hot liquid is then stirred into the gelatin to dissolve all granules completely. Gelatin mixtures chill more quickly in a metal bowl or mold than in a glass or pottery bowl or mold.

☐ *Which fruits added to gelatin desserts float and which ones sink?*

Fruits that float include fresh apples, bananas, grapefruit, melon balls, oranges, strawberries; canned mandarin oranges; frozen melon balls, peaches, raspberries and strawberries. Fruits that sink include fresh grapes, canned apricots, Bing cherries and pears.

☐ *How do I unmold gelatin desserts without melting them?*

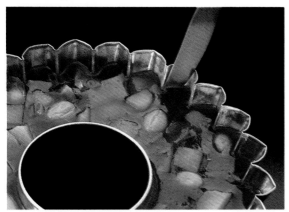

When set, remove gelatin from mold by loosening edge with tip of knife and dipping the mold, just to the edge, into warm water. Place a plate on top of the mold, and holding both tightly, invert plate and mold. Shake gently until gelatin slips onto serving dish.

**Meringues** are slow-baked, delicate shells made from a stiffly beaten mixture of egg whites, sugar and cream of tartar. The shells can be flavored and served with fillings of ice cream, custard, whipped cream, crushed fruit and toppings or a combination of these.

## Problems and Solutions

☐ *How can I be sure my baked meringues will be crisp?*

Follow a specific recipe for perfect, crisp meringues. It is best to bake them on a dry day because humid weather causes lower volume and less crisp shells.

☐ *How should I store baked meringues?*

Store baked meringue shells in airtight containers at room temperature or well wrapped in the freezer. Meringues that have softened can be heated in a 200°F oven until crisp.

**Soufflés** are light, baked desserts with a cream or fruit base plus beaten egg whites.

## Problem and Solution

☐ *Is there a way to prevent my dessert soufflés from collapsing?*

Beat egg whites, sugar and cream of tartar mixture until very stiff and glossy. Do not underbeat or overfold. Soufflés must be served immediately after removal from the oven or they will collapse.

# Eggs

Perfectly cooked eggs are tender, never tough or overdone. Poach, fry or soft-cook eggs over low heat; scramble them over medium heat; and cook French omelets quickly over medium-high heat. Always watch timing closely.

## Problems and Solutions

□ *Is there a way to tell if eggs have been hard-cooked?*

Use a crayon to mark egg after cooking. To tell whether an egg has been cooked, spin it; if it wobbles instead of spinning, it is uncooked.

□ *How do I beat egg whites?*

Beat whites in a clean, dry bowl with a clean beater. Any yolk in the whites will prevent them from beating properly. A beaten white should more than triple in volume. Beat on high speed until stiff peaks form but the whites are not dry. Egg whites at room temperature beat to higher volume.

□ *How do I fold another mixture into beaten egg whites?*

Pour mixture over egg whites, cut down through the mixture, then slide the spatula across the bottom and up the side of the bowl. Rotate bowl ¼ turn and continue folding just until no streaks remain.

□ *How can I use extra egg whites or yolks?*

Use egg whites in angel food cake, boiled frosting, divinity, meringue and white cake. Use egg yolks in boiled dressing, egg pastry, hollandaise and other sauces, and custards. Add yolks and whites to scrambled eggs.

□ *How do I freeze raw eggs?*

Freeze egg whites in a plastic ice cube tray; remove to a plastic bag for storage. To measure, remember that 2 tablespoons of defrosted liquid egg white are equal to 1 fresh egg white. Thaw frozen egg whites in the refrigerator. Egg yolks require special treatment for freezing. If the yolks are to be used in scrambled eggs or egg pastry, add ⅛ teaspoon salt for each ¼ cup of egg yolks. If the yolks are to be used in custards or sweet sauces, add 1½ teaspoons sugar or 1½ teaspoons corn syrup for each ¼ cup of egg yolks.

□ *Can I freeze cooked eggs?*

Hard-cooked egg yolks can be frozen successfully, but hard-cooked whites become tough and watery.

□ *Is there a substitute for fresh eggs?*

Liquid egg products, purchased frozen, can be substituted for whole eggs. They contain 80 percent egg white, and the yolks are replaced with nonfat milk, vegetable oils and other ingredients. Thaw and store egg substitutes in the refrigerator.

☐ *How can I make hard-cooked eggs easier to peel?*

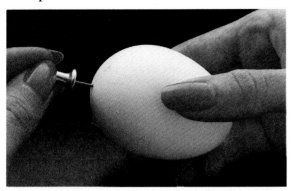

**Eggs** that are very fresh when hard-cooked are less difficult to peel if you pierce the large ends of eggs with an egg piercer, thumbtack or pin before hard-cooking. The small amount of water that may seep in during cooking makes egg peeling easier and also may keep the egg shell from cracking during cooking.

**Cool** eggs immediately in a bowl of cold water after cooking.

**To remove** shell easily, just tap egg to crackle shell; roll between hands to loosen shell, then peel. Hold egg under running cold water to help ease off shell.

☐ *How do I make a perfect omelet?*

**Stir** eggs quickly, sliding skillet back and forth over heat.

**Tilt** skillet; fold nearest omelet edge to center.

**Turn** onto plate; far side flips over onto unfolded portion.

# Fats & Oils

All fats and oils are not alike nor are they interchangeable in cooking and baking. Choose the best and most economical for every use; then store and handle each with care.

## Fats

### Problems and Solutions

☐ *What can I use as a substitute for butter, margarine or shortening?*

It is always best to follow the recipe exactly, but in many recipes calling for butter, margarine can be substituted in equal amounts. Do not substitute diet or whipped margarine in recipes calling for regular (stick) margarine because the diet or whipped kind has lower fat content and greater volume.

☐ *How do I clarify drippings from bacon and other meats for reuse?*

Pour drippings into a container through a funnel lined with a paper coffee filter; cover and refrigerate.

## Oils

### Problems and Solutions

☐ *All oils look the same, what is the difference from one to the other?*

**Corn** oil has a high smoke point, making it a good choice for frying, and a bland flavor, making it suitable for salad dressings.

**Olive** oil is pressed from fully ripened black olives. The first pressing is sold as virgin oil, is golden yellow in color and is used for salads, mayonnaise and frying. Subsequent pressings of the olives yield a less delicate oil.

**Peanut** oil has very little odor and no flavor and is used for salads, mayonnaise and frying.

**Safflower** oil is deep golden in color and high in polyunsaturated fatty acids; it is used in diet salad dressings and in low-cholesterol diets.

**Sesame** oil ranges from pale yellow to brown in color, may be odorless to aromatic and is used for cooking, salads and in Chinese cooking.

**Soybean** oil has many uses, ranging from salad dressings to cooking fats and margarines. It may have a strong flavor when heated.

**Vegetable** oil is an economical blend of oils from various vegetables; it has a bland flavor and a high smoke point, making it suitable for frying.

☐ *Which oils are best for deep-fat frying?*

Corn oil and vegetable oil are the best choices because both have higher smoke points than peanut or sesame oil. Soybean oil foams when used for deep-fat frying; olive oil has a low smoke point.

☐ *Can I substitute oil for other shortenings?*

Use oil only when called for in a recipe. Do not substitute it for other shortenings, even melted shortenings, because recipes formulated with shortening need the solids for proper structure and texture.

☐ *How do I prevent fats and oils from becoming rancid?*

Store lard and home-rendered fats in the refrigerator. Vegetable shortening can be stored at room temperature for short periods but should be refrigerated for storage of several months or more. Oils should be tightly capped and stored at room temperature or in the refrigerator. Olive oil becomes cloudy when refrigerated but becomes clear when returned to room temperature.

# Flours

Today bakeries, supermarkets and cookbooks abound in breads and pastries of many tastes and textures. The flours from which they are made differ widely, and each imparts special qualities to the finished product.
Knowing the correct variety of flour to use is an important secret in successful bread and cake baking.

**All-purpose** (1) is the name given to flour made from a blend of selected wheats and suitable for all kinds of baking. Bleached or unbleached, this flour can be used for most household cooking, including yeast breads, quick breads, pastries, cookies and cakes.

**Bread** flour is a special blend of wheats higher in protein than the wheats in all-purpose flour. Bread flour absorbs greater quantities of water and produces a more elastic dough than all-purpose flour. It is excellent for yeast-bread baking.

**Buckwheat** flour is obtained from sifting buckwheat meal ground from roasted seeds. It is used for pancakes, noodles and combined with all-purpose flour for making bread.

**Cake** flour is milled from soft wheat to produce a flour that produces tender, fine-textured cakes. Cake flour should be spooned into a measuring cup and then leveled.

**Instant or quick-mixing** (2) flour is an enriched all-purpose flour in granular form. This flour pours freely, is dust-free and blends very readily with liquid. It is used in main dishes, gravies and sauces and makes excellent popovers. Instant flour also can be used in cakes, breads and pastry, although batters and doughs made from it may look and feel different from those made with other flours.

**Rye** (3) flour is milled from rye grain and can be purchased in grades of white, medium and dark flour. Rye flour is combined with wheat flour in bread recipes because wheat flour produces gluten of greater elasticity.

**Self-rising** flour contains special kinds of leavening ingredients and salt for convenience in measuring and mixing to produce light biscuits and tender cakes.

**Soy** flour is ground from whole raw soybeans, has a slightly sweet taste and is combined with wheat flour in baked products because soy flour lacks gluten-forming proteins.

**Whole wheat** (4) flour, also called graham flour, is made from the complete wheat kernel. Stone-ground whole wheat flour is coarser than roller-milled whole wheat flour. Yeast bread made with all whole wheat has a nutty flavor and a dense texture; recipes for lighter loaves combine whole wheat flour with all-purpose flour.

# Fruits

The brilliant colors and distinctive tastes of fruit bring refreshment and nearly endless variety to menus. To enjoy them at their peak of flavor and freshness, learn to select, ripen, store and serve them properly.

## Apples

Apples should be firm to the touch and free from bruises. Choose specific varieties according to how they will be used.

**Baking:** Choose Granny Smith, Greening, Pippin, Starr and Rome Beauty.

**Pies:** Choose Cortland, Rhode Island, Greening, McIntosh and Yellow Transparent.

**Eating:** Choose Delicious, McIntosh, Jonathan and Winesap.

Apples can be used raw in salads, baked or used in pies and sauces.

*Tip:* To prevent apple slices from browning, toss them with lemon juice or dip into salted water immediately after slicing.

## Apricots

Choose plump, golden yellow fruit with velvetlike skin.

Apricots can be eaten fresh or used in salads, pies, jams and jellies.

## Avocados

Avocados come in varying shades of green and may have either smooth or "pebbly" skin. They usually are purchased as firm, unripened fruits and you can ripen them by leaving at room temperature for a few days. They are ripe when the flesh yields to a gentle pressure of your finger.

*Tip:* Ripening time can be shortened by placing the fruit in a slightly closed paper or plastic bag and leaving at room temperature.

*Tip:* To serve, cut fruit into halves, remove seed, peel off skin and slice. Sprinkle slices with lemon juice to prevent browning.

*Tip:* To make avocado shells, cut avocado lengthwise into halves, twisting gently to separate. To take out the seed, strike a knife directly into the seed and twist to lift it out. Fill center with seafood or chicken salad.

## Bananas

Purchase bananas that are yellow or yellow tipped with green and free from bruises. All-yellow bananas and those freckled with small brown specks are ripe and ready to eat. The banana can be used in breads and for desserts, and the greenish plantain as a vegetable.

*Tip:* Sprinkle lemon juice on banana slices to prevent discoloration.

# Blackberries

Choose large, dark, shiny berries. They are soft to the touch when ripe. Check the bottom of the container for juice stains that indicate injured or moldy fruit.

Blackberries can be eaten with cream and sugar. They are also suitable for pies, preserves and wine.

# Blueberries

Choose dark blue berries with a silvery cast. They should be round, firm and uniform in size. Avoid containers with juice-stained bottoms which indicate bruised berries.

Blueberries can be eaten with cream or cereal. They are good in jams, pies, fruit salads, sauces and quick breads.

# Cherries, sweet

Choose cherries that are plump with dark red-colored skins and green stems. Do not buy soft or shriveled fruits.

Cherries can be used for jams, pies, desserts, salads and garnishes.

# Coconuts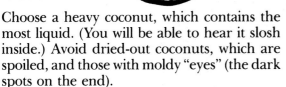

Choose a heavy coconut, which contains the most liquid. (You will be able to hear it slosh inside.) Avoid dried-out coconuts, which are spoiled, and those with moldy "eyes" (the dark spots on the end).

Coconut can be used fresh or toasted, can be eaten raw, baked in cookies, cakes and pies or used as a garnish.

*Tip:* To open a coconut, pierce the dark spots (eyes) with an ice pick or other suitable sharp object. Pour out the coconut milk. To break the shell, freeze coconut for about 1 hour. Remove from freezer; hit sharply in the middle with hammer. The coconut will separate easily from the shell. Store chunks of coconut, covered, in the refrigerator. Shred or slice to use in recipes or to eat.

# Cranberries

Cranberries are usually sold in plastic bags. Look for shiny, firm, red, plump berries. Avoid dull, soft and/or shriveled fruits.

Be sure to wash thoroughly and discard bad or bruised berries. Chop or grind cranberries for relish, cook for sauces, bake in pies or use as a garnish.

# Currants

Currants are small black seedless grapes that have been dried. They can be used in fruitcake, cookies and puddings.

## Dates

Choose plump, golden brown dates with smooth skins; avoid sticky dates.

*Tip:* Remove pits before using in breads, cakes and cookies. Cut dates with scissors dipped in water. Dates are a "natural candy."

## Figs

Figs grow in a variety of shapes with varying colors of skin and flesh (white, green, brown and purple). Figs must be tree-ripened, but squashed or overripe fruits should be avoided. Purchase figs at their peak of ripeness. Ripeness can be determined by softness; overripe figs have a sour aroma.

Eat fresh figs at room temperature because chilling subdues flavor. Also use figs for salads, cakes and garnishes. Figs are a popular dessert eaten alone or with cream.

## Gooseberries

Choose soft, ripe, light green-colored berries.

Gooseberries are usually too sour for eating raw; they are better when used for pies, jam and jelly.

## Grapefruit

Grapefruit are ripe when picked. Select heavy, firm fruits with thin, smooth skins which indicate a juicy fruit. Avoid fruits with pointed ends and/or rough skin, which indicate dryness. Choose between white or pink and seed or seedless grapefruits.

Pare and section to use in salads. Slice into halves at breakfast time or broil a half with brown sugar or grenadine for dessert.

## Grapes

Choose plump, slightly soft grapes that are well attached to green stems. Color indicates ripeness. Dark varieties should have no green, and green (white) grapes should have a yellowish amber cast.

Eat grapes with cheese, in salads, with meats or fish or use as a garnish.

## Guavas

Guavas can vary from small, walnut-sized fruits to large, apple-sized ones. A ripe guava has a green or yellow skin, depending on variety with white, yellow, pink or dark red flesh.

Serve guavas raw in salads or use for jelly, pies and sauces.

## Kiwi Fruit

Choose plump, undamaged fruits. They are ready to eat when fruit yields to slight pressure. The average kiwi fruit is the size of a large egg and weighs about 4 ounces.

Cut kiwi fruit into halves and eat with a spoon, or peel off the furry brown skin and slice. Use as a garnish, in salads or for desserts.

*Tip:* A slice of kiwi fruit rubbed on tough meat tenderizes it.

# Kumquats

Choose firm orange fruit.

Eat whole fruit, skin and all; use for preserves, jellies and candied fruit.

# Lemons

Choose lemons with smooth skins; avoid fruits with blemishes and/or soft spots. A dark yellow color indicates an older lemon, which has slightly less acid.

Grate the lemon peel for use in pies, cakes and cookies. Cut into wedges to squeeze over fish or use as a garnish. Lemon juice is used for beverages, pies and salad dressings. A few drops will enhance the flavor of nearly all bland foods.

*Tip:* To extract more juice from a lemon, do one of the following before squeezing:

▶ Microwave lemon on 50% power 1½ minutes.

▶ Using some pressure, roll the lemon back and forth 10 times on a hard surface.

▶ Soak the lemon in hot water for 30 minutes.

# Limes

Choose firm green limes with smooth skins. There are two basic varieties: Persian — large and greenish yellow; and Mexican — small and round (key limes).

Wedges of lime can be used as a garnish or squeezed over fish. Juice can be made into beverages, pies and frozen desserts, and lime peel is used for marmalade.

# Lychees

A mature lychee (nut) is shaped like a large strawberry with a scaly, brownish gray shell. Avoid shriveled fruits; lychees become nuts when dried.

Lychees are often served as an accompaniment to duck and pork, in Chinese dishes or cooked in syrup for dessert.

# Mangoes

Choose fruits that are slightly soft. They should be red, gold or flecked with some green. Avoid hard, all-green mangoes and very soft ones with black spots. Size will vary.

Mangoes are usually eaten fresh — sliced or with a spoon for breakfast, or as a dessert. They also can be pickled, made into preserves or chutney.

# Melons (See also Watermelon, page 61)

These general rules apply to all melons except watermelons: Choose firm, heavy melons with good color, distinctive aroma and smooth stem ends. (Attached stem indicates melon was picked too early.) Avoid soft or bruised melons. Sloshing sound inside indicates fruit is overripe.

Cut melon into pieces lengthwise or crosswise and remove seeds. Melon is frequently used in fruit salads and sliced and served with prosciutto ham as an appetizer.

*Tip:* Place ripe melon in plastic bag for storage in refrigerator to contain strong melon aromas, such as that of cantaloupe.

# Nectarines

Choose plump, slightly firm fruit that is creamy yellowish orange with a red blush. Avoid fruits that are shriveled, bruised or green at the stem end.

Nectarines are most flavorful when served at room temperature. Well-washed nectarines need not be peeled before eating. Use as a garnish, slice over cold cereal or use in recipes in place of peaches. Nectarines can be canned, frozen or preserved.

# Oranges

Choose seedless navel oranges for eating or Valencia oranges for juice. Oranges are ripe when picked, even if greenish in color. Select smooth-skinned fruit without blemishes. Heavy oranges are juicier than those lighter in weight.

*Tip:* To section, pare orange with a sharp knife down to the flesh; cut segments from between walls of membrane.

# Papayas

Choose fruits with smooth skin. Color, which indicates degree of ripeness, may range from the very green (unripe) to almost all yellowish orange (completely ripe). Avoid papayas with bruises or dark spots.

Slice papayas lengthwise into halves and remove seeds. Eat from the shell with a spoon, or pare and slice for salads and garnishes.

# Peaches

Select peaches that are firm or only slightly soft when pressed. The background color should be creamy or yellow. Avoid bruised, very hard or green peaches.

*Tip:* To peel, place peach in boiling water for 30 seconds; remove with a slotted spoon and plunge into iced water. The skin will come off easily. To prevent sliced fruit from discoloring, sprinkle with lemon juice.

# Pears

Because pears are picked before ripening for improved flavor and texture, select fruits that are still slightly firm. Avoid dull, shriveled fruits. Look for summer pears, such as Bartlett, from July to November and for winter pears, such as D'Anjou, Bosc and Comice, from October to May.

# Persimmons

Choose plump, bright orange fruits; color does not indicate ripeness. Fruits must be soft to be ripe and sweet; hard persimmons are very astringent in flavor.

Cut off stem end and eat with a spoon or pare and slice into wedges. Serve with cream or use in salads, cakes, cookies and puddings.

1. Crenshaw
2. Honeydew
3. Spanish melon
4. Mangoes
5. Papaya
6. Quince
7. Persimmon
8. Plantain
9. Bosc pears
10. Comice
11. Kiwi fruit
12. Gooseberries
13. Pomegranate
14. Kumquats
15. Figs
16. Nectarines

# Pineapples

Choose plump, slightly firm fruit with green leaves. It should be fragrant and sweet in flavor. Avoid bruised, dry or old fruit with browning leaves and soft spots.

*Tip:* To cut up a pineapple; Twist top from pineapple; cut pineapple into quarters. Holding pineapple securely, cut fruit from rind. Cut off pineapple core and remove "eyes." Slice lengthwise; cut into chunks, spears or grate.

*Tip:* Tenderize meat in fresh or frozen (thawed) pineapple juice; the enzyme bromelain that it contains breaks down the protein in the meat.

*Tip:* Do not add fresh pineapple or its juice to gelatin because the enzyme bromelain prevents jelling.

# Plums

Choose firm fruit that has good color. A slight softness at the tip indicates ripeness. Avoid plums that are hard, of bad color, bruised or very soft.

Use unpeeled plums for pies, desserts, garnishes, jams and jellies. They also can be canned or frozen.

# Pomegranates

Choose a full, heavy pomegranate with a smooth, unbruised rind. The larger the fruit, the bigger and juicier are the seeds. Avoid dry-looking pomegranates.

Use pomegranate seeds in salads or as a garnish; use juice from seeds in tropical drinks. To remove seeds, cut down 1 inch through rind at stem end; break into halves. Repeat cuts on halves; break into quarters. Pull back rind and separate seeds from membrane.

# Quinces

Choose firm, smooth, light yellow fruits of the largest available size.

Quinces are usually not eaten raw; they are used for jellies, preserves and pies.

# Raisins

Thompson seedless grapes are dried into two familiar types of raisins: sun-dried dark raisins and indoor-dried golden raisins, which are slightly larger and sweeter.

Raisins are used in yeast breads, fruitcakes, puddings and stuffings.

*Tip:* Plump raisins by covering the amount needed with very hot tap water and soaking two to five minutes. Drain well before using. (Raisins in liquid batters do not need to be plumped.) Longer soaking results in flavor and nutrient loss.

# Raspberries

Choose plump berries of dusky medium red color and with no stems attached. To avoid buying crushed, mushy, overripe berries, check the bottom of the container for staining.

Raspberries can be used in cordials, jams, jellies, frozen desserts and pies.

# Rhubarb

Choose rhubarb that has firm, crisp stalks and fresh-looking leaves, if any. Color varies from the light pink of hothouse-grown rhubarb to the deep red of field-grown fruit. Almost never eaten raw, rhubarb can be stewed, baked in pies, preserved in jams or frozen.

*Tip:* To cut up rhubarb, first remove the toxic leaves, which contain oxalic acid. Unlike the tender hothouse-grown variety, field-grown rhubarb must be peeled to remove tough fibers before slicing.

# Strawberries

Choose large or medium-sized plump, bright red berries that have fresh green caps. Avoid strawberries with white spots, a dry appearance or mold. Use fresh strawberries for jams, jellies, pies and desserts.

*Tip:* To remove caps, twist off or cut out with the point of a paring knife. Or leave caps on and dip strawberries into powdered sugar or orange-flavored liqueur.

# Tangerines

Tangerines are a type of mandarin orange. Choose fruits with clear orange color and shiny skins. Since their skins are naturally loose, tangerines will not feel firm. Avoid fruits with soft spots or breaks in the skin.

The loose skin is easily peeled off; the segments separate easily. Eat as a snack or use in salads, desserts and for garnishes.

# Watermelons

Choose a whole watermelon by its color. A yellowish underside and velvetlike appearance indicate ripeness. Select crisp, juicy-looking watermelon wedges with dark seeds.

Slice and eat. Use for snacks, desserts and salads. The pared rind can be used for pickles.

To make a watermelon basket, use a knife tip to score a band halfway down each side from center top for handle. Turn knife; score horizontally around melon. Cut two pieces away from handle. Scoop out melon from under the handle and from base. Fill basket with fruit, including the melon.

# Garnishes

Edible garnishes, simple or complicated, add color and elegance to food. Garnish is not synonymous with parsley. Many fruits and vegetables, cheese and eggs can be used to add texture and eye appeal to plain food. Whatever the garnish you choose, it should be small and not a hindrance to carving meat or serving food. Clean or wash, cut and chill garnishes ahead of time so they will be ready when needed.

## Butter, Cheese and Egg

**Butter balls,** (1) made with wooden butter paddles, can be shaped ahead and refrigerated or frozen until needed.

**Butter curls**, made with a butter curler, can be made ahead and refrigerated in iced water.

**Butter fancies,** (2) formed in butter molds or by pushing softened butter through a cake decorating tube onto a cookie sheet, can be frozen and packaged for future use.

**Butter pats** can be made by cutting a ¼-pound stick of firm butter with a wire butter cutter or knife. Top each pat with a sprig of parsley, if desired, and refrigerate.

**Cheese strips** (3) can be arranged in a criss-cross pattern on cold salads or hot vegetables just before serving.

**Hard-cooked eggs**, sliced, quartered or chopped, can be used to top salads, casseroles or thick soups.

## Fruit

**Spiced red crab apples** or spiced apple rings topped with mint jelly are colorful garnishes for pork or roast lamb.

**Spiced or dried apricots**, pears or peaches can form an attractive ring around a platter of sliced meat.

**Green and purple grapes** can be used to encircle a platter of lamb.

**Lemon or orange slices** (4) can be cut just to centers and twisted with parsley tucked between twists.

**Edges of lemon wedges** (5) can be dipped in paprika or cinnamon and served with seafood.

**Lime or lemon flowers** (6) can be made by cutting a thin slice from stem end, cutting around the fruit without removing knife to form spiral of peel and curling peel onto base to resemble flower.

**Orange half**, with pulp removed, can be filled with cranberry relish to serve with poultry.

**Orange slices,** cut thick, can be studded on edges with whole cloves or can be notched with kitchen scissors and served with roast duck or pork.

**Peach halves** can be filled with chutney and heated to serve with ham.

**Pear halves** can be heated, filled with mint jelly and served with lamb.

# Vegetable

**Carrot curls** can be made by cutting paper-thin slices of carrot lengthwise with vegetable parer, rolling up slices, securing with picks and chilling in iced water to serve with sandwiches or garnish salads.

**Carrot daisies** (9) can be made by cutting carrot into thin slices; cut out circles with scalloped or round cutter. Make V-shaped notches around plain circles to form petals. Attach thin slice of black olive to center of each circle with dab of cream cheese to form daisy center.

**Celery sticks** (7) can be slit from each end almost to center and chilled in iced water to curl, then used to decorate a platter of sliced cold meat.

**Green pepper and red onion** (8) can be sliced thinly and arranged alternately around a platter of roast beef.

**Mushrooms** (11) can be given a spiral pattern by cutting 5 curved double slits from center to outer edge on rounded side of large mushroom and removing small wedge of mushroom between cuts. Serve with fish. You might also look for flat or open mushrooms which are large with a strong flavor, dark brown "veil" and used in cooking. Enokitake, a Japanese tree mushroom with long stems and tiny caps, have a mild flavor and are used in salads, as a garnish or in cooking.

**Parsley sprigs** or snippets will stay crisp and green 1 month or longer if rinsed under cold water, shaken free of excess moisture and refrigerated in tightly covered glass jar.

**Pickle fans** (10) can be made by cutting lengthwise slits almost to end of a small pickle then spreading apart. Serve with grilled hamburgers or use to garnish a platter of meat.

**Radish roses** or rosettes can be made by cutting radishes into petals and chilling in iced water until petals open. Use to garnish cold sliced meat.

**Vegetable kabobs** (12) can be made by alternating thin slices of pickles and raw vegetables of contrasting colors on wooden picks to garnish hot dogs or hamburgers.

**Zucchini rings** can be made by removing center of zucchini with apple corer before slicing. Use as a garnish for broiled fish.

# Grains

Important staple foods that come in many forms, grains are the basic ingredient in breads and baked goods. Grains add flavor, texture and nutrients to foods.

**1. Bulgur** is also known as parboiled wheat or wheat pilaf. Whole wheat is cooked and dried, part of the bran is removed and the remaining grain is cracked into coarse, angular fragments that retain their shape and chewy eating quality after cooking. Bulgur is used in salads or cooked in broth and served with chicken or lamb.

**2. Cornmeal** is made from grinding white or yellow corn and is used in breads, muffins, fried mush and pudding.

**3. Cracked wheat** is grain that has been crushed to a coarse texture between rollers rather than having been ground. It is baked into bread, adding chewiness and visible whole-grain flecks.

**4. Grits** are meal that has been coarsely ground from hulled kernels of corn. They can be cooked and eaten as breakfast cereal or served as a side dish to smoked meat.

**5. Kasha** is the seed of buckwheat, barley or millet that has been boiled, dried and coarsely ground. Kasha is also called buckwheat groats and is a staple in eastern European cooking; it is served as a hearty side dish to meat, poultry and game.

**6. Oats** are sometimes called quick-cooking in recipes. Oats have been hulled, softened and flattened by rollers. Quick-cooking oats are thinner than regular oats. Both can be baked into cookies and breads or used as extenders for meat loaf.

**7. Wheat germ** is the embryo of the wheat kernel, which is flattened into a yellowish oily flake. It is usually toasted for nutlike flavor. It can be used as a cereal topping or baked into breads, cookies and desserts.

# Herbs, Seeds & Spices

Herbs and spices are nature's gifts to the good cook. Used discriminately, they enhance rather than overwhelm foods with their flavors and fragrances. The chart below is a general guide to selecting the herbs, aromatic seeds and spices that are compatible with certain foods. To have fresh herbs always at hand, follow the directions for growing them indoors (page 70). (See also Storings Foods, page 149)

| How to Select and Use Herbs, Seeds and Spices | | | | |
| --- | --- | --- | --- | --- |
| Name and Type | Country of Origin | Flavor | Form(s) | Use in Cooking |
| Allspice (spice) | Jamaica | combination of cloves, cinnamon and nutmeg | whole, ground | cakes, cookies, fruits, pickling, pies, stews |
| Anise seed (aromatic seed) | Spain | licorice | whole, ground | cakes, candies, liqueur, rolls, salads |
| Basil (herb) | United States, Europe | sweet, with clovelike pungent tang | dried leaves, ground | eggs, meats, salads, soups, stews, tomato dishes |
| Bay leaves (herb) | Greece, Italy, Turkey | pungent, aromatic | dried leaves, ground | meats, pickling, sauces, soups, stews, vegetables |
| Caraway seed (aromatic seed) | Holland | intense, aromatic | whole, seeds | cabbage, cheese, meats, pickling, rye bread, sauerkraut, soups, stews |
| Cardamom (aromatic seed) | Guatemala, India | pungent with slight menthol flavor | whole pod, seeds, ground | coffee, custard, curry, fruit, sausages, Scandinavian breads |
| Cayenne pepper (spice) | United States, West Africa | very hot, peppery | ground | eggs, fish, gravies, meats, sauces, vegetables |
| Celery seed (aromatic seed) | France | concentrated celery flavor, slightly bitter | whole, ground | dressings, meats, pickling, salads, sauces, soups, stuffings |
| Chervil (herb) | United States, France | more aromatic than parsley with slight anise flavor | dried leaves | eggs, fish, salads, sauces, soups, stuffings |

## How to Select and Use Herbs, Seeds and Spices

| Name and Type | Country of Origin | Flavor | Form(s) | Use in Cooking |
|---|---|---|---|---|
| Chili powder (blend of chili peppers, cumin, coriander, garlic and onion powder, oregano, cloves, allspice or other spices) | United States | spicy, hot | ground | cocktail sauces, cottage cheese, eggs, Mexican dishes, soups, stews, vegetables |
| Chives (herb) | United States | onionlike | freeze-dried | appetizers, cream soups, eggs, garnishes, salads |
| Cinnamon (spice) | China, Indonesia, Java, Sumatra | aromatic, pungent, sweet | stick, ground | cakes, cookies, fruit desserts, pies, pickling, puddings |
| Cloves (spice) | Malagasy Republic (Madagascar), Tanzania | aromatic, strong, pungent, sweet | whole, ground | desserts, fruit, ham, gravies, meats, pickling, pork, sausages, stews, syrups, vegetables |
| Coriander (aromatic seed) | Argentina, France, Morocco, Yugoslavia | mildly fragrant, similar to a cross between lemon peel and sage | whole, ground | breads, cakes, cookies, curry powder, sausages, seafood, Mexican and Spanish dishes, pickling, pastries |
| Cumin (aromatic seed) | Middle East, Morocco | pungent, savory, slightly bitter | whole, ground | cheese, pickling, pork, sauerkraut |
| Curry powder (blend of many ground spices) | India | pungent, hot to mild | ground | eggs, fish, meats, sauces, vegetables |
| Dill seed (aromatic seed) | United States, India | tangy, similar to caraway | whole, ground | fish, meats, pickling, processed meats, salads, sauces, soups |
| Dill weed (herb) | United States | pungent | whole, dried | breads, cheese, fish, salads, sauces, vegetables |
| Fennel seed (aromatic seed) | Argentina, India | aromatic, sweet, resembles licorice | whole, ground | breads, fish, Italian dishes, sauces, sausages, soups, sweet pickles |

## How to Select and Use Herbs, Seeds and Spices

| Name and Type | Country of Origin | Flavor | Form(s) | Use in Cooking |
|---|---|---|---|---|
| Fenugreek (aromatic seed) | Argentina, France, India, Lebanon | maple flavor with currylike aroma | whole, ground | chutney, curry powder, imitation maple flavoring |
| Garlic (dehydrated) (See Vegetables, page 120) | United States | pungent aroma and taste | minced, powdered | fish, meats, salads, sauces, sausages, soups, vegetables |
| Ginger (spice) | Jamaica, Sierra Leone, India | pungent, spicy | whole, cracked (bits), ground | fish, fruits, meats, sauces, sausages, soups, vegetables |
| Horseradish (dehydrated) | United States | pungent | powdered | appetizers, meats, salads, sauces, stews |
| Mace (spice) | Indochina, East Indies, West Indies | intense, similar to nutmeg | ground | cakes, chocolate, fish, fruit, desserts, salads, soups |
| Marjoram (herb) | France, Peru, Chile, North Africa | aromatic with slightly bitter overtone | dried leaves, ground | cottage cheese, fish, lamb, poultry, sausages, soups, stews, stuffings, vegetables |
| Mint (herb) | Belgium, France, Germany | strong, sweet with cool aftertaste | dried leaves, flakes | beverages, desserts, fish, lamb, sauces, soups |
| Mustard (aromatic seed) | United States, Canada, Denmark, England | hot, pungent with dry aftertaste | whole seed, ground | casseroles, meats, pickling, relishes, salads, vegetables |
| Nutmeg (spice) | Indochina, East Indies, West Indies | fragrant, sweet with spicy undertone | whole, ground | beverages, cakes, cookies, puddings, sauces, vegetables |
| Oregano (herb) | Dominican Republic, Greece, Italy, Sicily | strong, aromatic with pleasantly bitter undertone | dried leaves, ground | cheese, eggs, fish, Italian dishes, meats, sauces, soups, vegetables |
| Paprika (spice) | California, South America, Spain, Eastern Europe | slightly bitter, ranges from sweet to hot | ground | casseroles, eggs, fish, garnish, meats, salads, soups, vegetables |
| Parsley (herb) | Mediterranean, United States | slightly peppery | fresh, dried leaves | garnish, herb mixtures, sauces, stews, soup |

## How to Select and Use Herbs, Seeds and Spices

| Name and Type | Country of Origin | Flavor | Form(s) | Use in Cooking |
|---|---|---|---|---|
| Pepper (spice) | Brazil, India, Indonesia, Malaysia | hot, biting and very pungent | whole, ground | casseroles, eggs, meats, pickling, salads, sausages, soups, vegetables |
| Poppy seed (aromatic seed) | Netherlands, Poland, Argentina, France, Germany | pleasant, nutlike | whole | topping for breads, cakes, cookies, fillings for pastries |
| Rosemary (herb) | United States, France, Spain, Yugoslavia, Portugal | fresh, sweet flavor | dried leaves | casseroles, fish, lamb, salads, seafood, soups, vegetables |
| Saffron (spice) | Spain | softly bitter, distinctive flavor | dried strands, powdered | poultry, rice, rolls, sauces, seafood, Spanish dishes |
| Sage (herb) | Yugoslavia | aromatic, slightly bitter | dried leaves, rubbed, ground | dressings, fish, meats, poultry, salads, sausages, soups, stuffings |
| Savory (herb) | France, Spain, Yugoslavia | aromatic, slightly pungent | dried leaves, ground | poultry, meats, salads, sauces, soups, stuffings, vegetables |
| Sesame seed (aromatic seed) | China, India, Turkey, Central America | rich, nutlike | whole | candies, cookies, garnish, topping for rolls, salads, pastries |
| Tarragon (herb) | United States, France | piquant, reminiscent of anise | dried leaves | eggs, meats, pickling, poultry, salads, sauces, tomatoes |
| Thyme (herb) | United States, France, Spain, Portugal | aromatic, pungent | dried leaves, ground | chowders, fish, meats, poultry, stews, stuffings, tomatoes |
| Turmeric (spice) | India, Haiti, Jamaica, Peru | aromatic, slightly bitter | ground | curry powder, eggs, food color, pickling, poultry, rice, seafood |

1. Fennel seed
2. Turmeric
3. Saffron
4. Rosemary
5. Anise seed
6. Freeze dried chives
7. Cayenne pepper
8. Coriander
9. Sage
10. Whole cloves
11. Bay leaves
12. Sesame seed
13. Cinnamon sticks
14. Whole nutmeg
15. Dill weed
16. Paprika

## Problems and Solutions

☐ *Which common herbs can be grown indoors during winter months?*

Basil, chervil, chives, marjoram, parsley, rosemary, sage, savory and thyme all can be grown indoors.

☐ *What are the secrets and techniques for growing herbs indoors?*

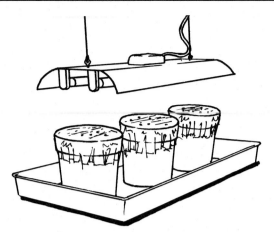

Herbs from seeds must be grown indoors under fluorescent light. Start by filling 5-inch-diameter clay pots to within ½ inch of top with seed-starting soil. Wet soil thoroughly; allow to drain well.

With a pencil or chopstick, make 2 furrows ⅛ to ¼ inch deep (depending on seed variety). The furrows should be even, parallel and 1½ inches apart.

Sprinkle seeds in the furrows; cover carefully with soil. Cover pots with plastic wrap; punch a few holes in the top for ventilation. Place pots in plastic tray.

Place tray under fluorescent light. The tops of pots should be about 8 inches from light. The fluorescent light should shine on the pots 14 to 16 hours each day.

When seedlings appear above the soil (7 to 14 days), remove plastic wrap. If seeds are slow to germinate and the soil appears dry, it may be necessary to remove plastic wrap and water seedlings with a plant mister. Avoid direct watering, which will wash out seeds.

When seedlings are 1 inch tall, thin with scissors so that plants are ½ inch apart. (Use the seedling cuttings for cooking.) Water seedlings when soil appears dry. In 6 to 8 weeks, plants will be large enough to grow in the window or plant in the garden.

□ *How can I preserve herbs by freezing?*

Wash and drain herbs; wrap in foil or place in plastic bag. Label packages and freeze. If you have several types of herbs, each in a small bag, store them all together in a plastic container or glass jar for easy locating.

□ *How can I preserve herbs by drying?*

Dry herbs as soon as possible after picking to retain color, flavor and fragrance. Large-leaved herbs (basil, mint and sage) should be removed from the stems and dried on a window screening or cheesecloth-covered frame. Small-leaved herbs can be dried in this manner, or they may be tied in small bunches and hung to dry. All drying should be done in a warm, dry, well-ventilated area, out of direct sunlight. When leaves are dry and crisp, remove from the stems, if necessary, and store in airtight containers.

□ *How can I grow mung bean sprouts?*

Fold a piece of terry cloth or cheesecloth (about 16 × 8 inches) into fourths (8 × 4 inches). Place in a loaf pan, 9 × 5 × 3 inches. Pour water over the cloth until it is saturated, then sprinkle ¼ cup dried green mung beans in a single layer on top. Cover pan with aluminum foil; let stand 24 hours. Uncover the pan and set it in a dark, draft-free place. Water it each day as the top layer dries out. Beans will sprout in 2 or 3 days and will be ready to harvest within 4 to 6 days.

To harvest, snip the plants off at the base with scissors. Use fresh or rinse to remove the husks and dry well. Place in a plastic bag; close tightly and refrigerate no longer than 3 days. The yield from ¼ cup dried mung beans is 3 cups.

□ *How can I prevent parsley and other fresh herbs from becoming limp and yellow during storage?*

Rinse fresh herbs in cold water after picking; shake well to remove excess water. Refrigerate in tightly covered glass container.

□ *How do I substitute fresh for dried herbs?*

Use three times the amount of finely chopped fresh herbs to substitute for dried herbs.

□ *How can I make my own bouquet garni?*

The traditional herbs in a bouquet garni are parsley, thyme and bay leaf. The proportion of each herb may vary with the type of food being prepared. The herbs either can be tied in cheesecloth or placed in a perforated tea ball to be conveniently removed at the end of cooking time.

□ *Dried herbs never seem to have as much flavor as I like; what can I do to increase their flavor?*

Dried herbs will have a stronger flavor if they are crushed between fingers before being added to food.

□ *How can I use dried herbs in sauces without having crunchy, dry flecks of them?*

Rehydrate dried herbs before adding to cold sauces or dips. Place herbs in boiling water for 30 seconds; strain, pat dry and add to sauces or dips.

□ *Is there a way to give dried herbs a fresh herb color?*

Add an equal amount of fresh, finely snipped parsley to dried herbs, such as basil, to give the herbs a fresh green color.

# Legumes

Legumes are dried beans, peas and lentils from pods containing one row of seeds.
They are an excellent source of vegetable protein, and
combined with small amounts of cheese and milk, provide complete protein.

## Problems and Solutions

☐ *If I don't have the dried beans called for in a recipe, can I substitute another kind?*

Beans can be used interchangeably; a similar type can be substituted in your recipe. The exception is lentils, which need no soaking and can be cooked in a shorter time. Because beans double or triple in volume as they cook, choose a sufficiently large casserole or pan.

☐ *Is there a quick way to soften dried beans or peas for cooking?*

Boil beans 2 minutes in sufficient water to cover. Remove from heat; cover and let stand 1 hour and they are ready to cook.

☐ *How do I prevent the cooking water from foaming when cooking dried beans?*

Add 1 tablespoon of oil or shortening during the first cooking period.

☐ *Can I cook dried beans, peas and legumes in the pressure cooker?*

Dried beans or whole peas can be cooked in the pressure cooker. Legumes that cook quickly, such as black-eyed peas, lentils or small lima beans, are not ordinarily pressure-cooked. Split peas should not be cooked in the pressure cooker because they foam during cooking and may clog the vent. Follow individual manufacturer's directions for exact cooking procedures.

## Common Types of Legumes

| Type | Color | Size and Shape | Use |
|---|---|---|---|
| 1. Black beans | black | small, oval | baked, soups, stews |
| 2. Black-eyed peas | white with a black spot | small, oval | casseroles |
| 3. Garbanzo beans (chick peas) | brown | small, irregular | dips, casseroles, salads, soups, stews |
| 4. Great Northern beans | white | medium, oval | baked, casseroles, chowder, soups, stews |
| 5. Kidney beans | red | medium, oval | casseroles, chili, salads, soups |
| 6. Lentils | brown or green | small, round disk | casseroles, salads, soups |
| 7. Lima beans | white | large, small, flat | casseroles, soups |
| 8. Navy beans | white | small, round | baked, soups |
| 9. Pinto beans | pink speckled with brown | medium, oval | casseroles, soups |
| 10. Red beans | red | small, round | casseroles, chili |
| 11. Soybeans | tan | small, round | casseroles, salads |
| 12. Split peas | green or yellow | small, round | soups |

# Marinades

Marinades are the wonder workers that can transform meat of commonplace flavor and doubtful tenderness into a memorable taste experience. The time-honored process of marinating is a natural one — bathing the meat (or other foods) in herbs, a tenderizer such as wine and oil before roasting or grilling.

**Lemon juice** and oil with herbs tenderize and season meat and vegetables.

**Soy sauce** combined with honey, garlic and herbs is sometimes called teriyaki marinade for meat and fish.

**Tomato** in the form of juice or sauce is an acid which, when combined with soy sauce, garlic, oil and seasonings, will tenderize tough meat, such as wild game, before cooking.

**Vinegar** and oil with herbs is sometimes called a vinaigrette marinade. A simple substitute is bottled vinegar and oil salad dressing for tenderizing meat or flavoring vegetables.

**Wine** (usually red) combined with oil, spices and garlic is sometimes used to marinate less tender steaks.

**Yogurt** can be used alone or combined with lemon juice and seasonings to flavor and tenderize chicken before grilling or baking.

## Problems and Solutions

☐ *What kind of container should I use for marinating food?*

Marinate food in a glass container because it is impervious to the acid in the marinade. Earthenware and metals other than stainless steel are not recommended because of their reactions to acids.

☐ *Can I use beer for marinating?*

Yes you can marinate meat or seafood in beer for several hours in the refrigerator to add flavor and tenderize food.

☐ *If I don't have enough marinade to completely cover the food, what should I do?*

Place meat or poultry in a heavy plastic bag, pour in marinade and secure top of bag; turn occasionally. The mariande will remain in contact with the meat and will penetrate crevices of poultry pieces

☐ *Where should meat, poultry or fish be stored while being marinated?*

Always store foods that are being marinated in the refrigerator, not at room temperature.

# Meats

Cuts of meat are often named for the bones they contain (rib roast, T-bone steak, arm pot roast, to name a few). Bone shape is also an indication of the tenderness of a specific cut of meat. Bones in beef, lamb, pork and veal are almost identical in appearance, and the 7 principal bone groups named below are sketched on the following two pages. They are all you need to identify cut and tenderness of meat. (Most other bones are removed before meat is packaged and sold.)

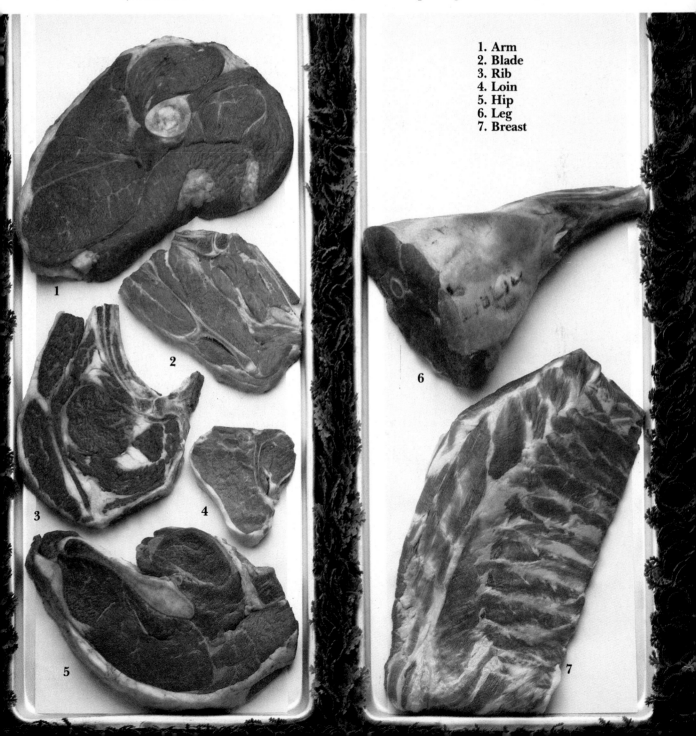

1. Arm
2. Blade
3. Rib
4. Loin
5. Hip
6. Leg
7. Breast

# Selecting and Cooking

The chart below is designed to take the mystery out of meat selection and cooking. Study the information in it for a simple way to identify cuts of meat, degree of tenderness and appropriate cooking method. Learn to choose for yourself and to talk knowledgeably to your meat dealer. Bones sketched below are shown in cuts of meat on the preceding page.

## How to Identify Cuts of Meat by the Bones

| Type of Bone | | Common Name | General Cooking Method (page 82) |
|---|---|---|---|
| **Arm** | | | |
| | | beef chuck arm steak | braise, cook in liquid |
| | | beef chuck arm pot roast | braise, cook in liquid |
| | | lamb shoulder arm chop | braise, broil, panfry |
| | | lamb shoulder arm roast | roast |
| | | pork shoulder arm steak | braise, panfry |
| | | pork shoulder arm roast | roast |
| | | veal shoulder arm steak | braise, panfry |
| | | veal shoulder arm roast | braise, roast |
| **Blade** center cuts | | | |
| | | beef chuck blade steak | braise, cook in liquid |
| | | beef chuck blade pot roast | braise, cook in liquid |
| | | lamb shoulder blade chop | braise, broil, panfry |
| | | lamb shoulder blade roast | roast |
| | | pork shoulder blade steak | braise, broil, panfry |
| | | pork shoulder blade Boston roast | braise, roast |
| | | veal shoulder blade steak | braise, panfry |
| | | veal shoulder blade roast | braise, roast |
| **Rib** back bone and rib bone | | | |
| | | beef rib steak | broil, panfry |
| | | beef rib roast | roast |
| | | lamb rib chop | broil, panfry |
| | | lamb rib roast | roast |
| | | pork rib chop | braise, broil, panfry |
| | | pork rib roast | roast |
| | | veal rib chop | braise, panfry |
| | | veal rib roast | roast |

## How to Identify Cuts of Meat by the Bones

| Type of Bone | Common Name | General Cooking Method (page 82) |
|---|---|---|
| **Loin** | | |
| back bone (T-shape) | beef loin steak (T-bone, porterhouse) | broil, panfry |
| | beef loin tenderloin roast or steak | roast, broil |
| | lamb loin chop | broil, panfry |
| | lamb loin roast | roast |
| | pork loin chop | braise, broil, panfry |
| | pork loin roast | roast |
| | veal loin chop | braise, panfry |
| | veal loin roast | roast, braise |
| **Hip** | | |
| pin bone (near short loin) | beef sirloin steak | broil, panfry |
| | beef loin tenderloin roast or steak | roast, broil |
| flat bone (center cuts) | lamb sirloin chop | broil, panfry |
| | lamb leg roast | roast |
| | pork sirloin chop | braise, broil, panfry |
| | pork sirloin roast | roast |
| wedge bone (near round) | veal sirloin steak | braise, panfry |
| | veal leg sirloin roast | roast |
| **Leg** | | |
| leg or round bone | beef round steak | braise, panfry |
| | beef rump roast | braise, roast |
| | lamb leg steak | broil, panfry |
| | lamb leg roast | roast |
| | pork leg (ham) steak | braise, broil, panfry |
| | pork leg roast (fresh or smoked) | roast |
| | veal leg round steak | braise, panfry |
| | veal leg roast | braise, roast |
| **Breast** | | |
| breast and rib | beef brisket (fresh or corned) | braise, cook in liquid |
| | beef plate short rib | braise, cook in liquid |
| | lamb breast | roast, braise |
| | lamb breast riblet | braise, cook in liquid |
| | pork bacon (side pork) | broil, panfry, bake |
| | pork sparerib | roast, braise, cook in liquid |
| | veal breast | roast, braise |
| | veal breast riblet | braise, cook in liquid |

## Problems and Solutions

*□ What is "beef-in-a-bag"?*

"Beef-in-a-bag" or boxed beef is a boneless section of beef, trimmed of excess fat, vacuum-packed at the processing plant and shipped to the supermarket in boxes. You can buy the whole bag of beef, cut steaks and roasts of whatever size you want, wrap and place in your freezer. Refer to page 83 for cutting and cooking instructions. Some supermarkets will do the cutting for you.

*□ What is "family pack" beef?*

Supermarkets feature family pack meats and poultry as a convenient and economical way for shoppers to buy an assortment of cuts packaged in single trays of various sizes.

*□ Why is prepackaged hamburger often red on the surface and greyish brown inside?*

A natural pigment in all beef combines with oxygen when exposed to air, producing the red exterior color of hamburger. The unexposed interior of the meat does not change color. The change in exterior color does not affect quality of flavor.

*□ How much fat is in "regular," "lean," and "extra lean" ground beef?*

Regular (1) (ground chuck) contains no more than 30 percent fat. Lean (2) (ground round) contains approximately 23 percent fat. Extra lean (3) (ground sirloin) contains approximately 15 percent fat.

*□ Is eating rare hamburger dangerous?*

No, hamburger can safely be eaten rare if it is cooked until inside color is at least brownish pink and internal temperature is 145°F.

*□ What is the safe internal temperature of properly cooked pork and ham?*

Fresh pork should be cooked to 170°F. Hams labeled "cook before eating" should be cooked to an internal temperature of 160°F. Hams labeled "fully cooked" can be eaten without further cooking. To serve fully cooked hams hot, heat to an internal temperature of 140°F. If a ham is not labeled, assume that it should be cooked before eating.

*□ How can I identify quality bacon?*

The best bacon is about ⅓ lean. Look for uniform slices of bacon with fine ribbons of lean throughout.

*□ Can I identify quality veal?*

Veal is a light grayish pink in color with a fine grain and fairly firm, velvety texture. Veal from calves up to 6 months of age has a small amount of white fat, and bones that are porous and red.

□ *What is meant by the term "genuine lamb"?*

As specified by the USDA, genuine lamb is meat that comes from sheep that are less than 1 year old.

□ *How can I identify quality lamb?*

Lamb that has fine-textured, reddish pink meat with very little marbling (flecks of fat within the lean) is the meat of a young animal. In addition, the meat of quality lamb has a smooth covering of brittle white fat.

□ *How can a leg of lamb be cut into pieces?*

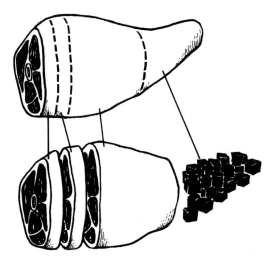

Two to 4 sirloin steaks can be cut from a three-quarter leg of lamb. This leaves a center roast of about 3 pounds and the shank portion, which can be cut into cubes or strips. The pieces can be wrapped and frozen for several meals of lamb cooked in a variety of ways.

□ *How can I keep veal from becoming dry after cooking?*

If a veal roast has little or no fat on the surface, top with 2 or 3 slices of bacon or salt pork before roasting. Or cook veal over medium heat or at an oven temperature of 325°F.

□ *How should meat be wrapped for storage in the freezer?*

**Place** meat on center of wrap; bring edges of wrap together above meat.

**Fold** wrap over once, then fold toward meat a second time so wrap is tight against meat.

**Fold** ends of wrap together and turn under package away from the top fold, sealing air out of package.

**Seal** with freezer tape and label package with contents and date.

## Variety Meats

| Type | Description | General Cooking Method (page 82) |
|---|---|---|
| **Brains** | beef, lamb, pork or veal; very tender and delicate in flavor | braise, panfry, precook in water to help keep and make firm |
| **Heart** | beef, lamb, pork or veal; less-tender than other variety meats; very flavorful | braise, cook in liquid, pressure-cook |
| **Kidney** | beef, lamb, pork or veal; beef kidney is less tender and stronger in flavor than other kidneys | braise, cook in liquid, broil more tender types |
| **Liver** | beef, lamb, pork or veal; beef liver is less tender than other livers; veal and lamb liver are milder in flavor than beef and pork liver | braise, panfry, broil |
| **Sweetbreads** | beef, lamb or veal; tender and delicately flavored | braise, panfry, cook in liquid |
| **Tongue** | beef, lamb, pork or veal; may be purchased fresh, pickled, corned, smoked or canned | cook in liquid, pressure-cook |
| **Tripe** | beef; purchase fresh, pickled, canned or precooked; honeycomb most delicately flavored | cook in liquid, then braise, panfry or broil |

Variety meats are more perishable than other types of meat; they should be refrigerated or frozen and used within 1 day of purchase and/or thawing.

## Sausages and Ready-to-Serve Meats

| Type | Description | Varieties (over 200 available) |
|---|---|---|
| 1. Cooked sausage | fresh ground seasoned meat in casings, cooked and ready to eat; usually served cold | beer salami, braunschweiger, liver sausage, veal sausage |
| 2. Cooked smoked sausage | fresh meat, cooked and smoked; ready to eat but heating before serving improves flavor | bologna, frankfurter (hot dog, wiener), kielbasa, knackwurst, smoked links, Vienna sausage |
| 3. Dry and semi-dry sausage | many varieties from selected meats, mild to highly seasoned, smoked or unsmoked; can be served uncooked | cervelat (farmer, Göteborg, Thüringer), Frizzes, pepperoni, salami (Genoa, hard), summer sausage |
| 4. Fresh sausage | primarily fresh ground or chopped pork and beef; cook thoroughly before serving | fresh beef sausage, bockwurst, bratwurst, country-style pork sausage, fresh pork sausage (large or small links) |
| 5. Fresh smoked sausage | fresh meats, cured or uncured, smoked; cook thoroughly before serving | smoked country-style pork sausage, mettwurst, Romanian sausage, smoked link sausage |
| 6. Ready-to-serve meats | commonly called luncheon meats, available presliced or in loaves; usually served cold | chopped ham, head cheese, honey loaf, luncheon meat, olive loaf, peppered loaf, pickle and pimiento loaf |

# General Cooking Methods

If you have bought cuts of meat at your super-market because they were specially priced or looked particularly good, you can identify them and determine cooking methods by re-ferring to page 76 (How to Identify Cuts of Meat by the Bone). If you do not have specific recipes for preparing them, follow these general cooking methods for meat.

**Roast** by placing meat, fat side up, on rack in open shallow roasting pan. If desired, sprinkle with salt and pepper or herbs before roasting. Add no water and do not cover. Roast in 325°F oven to desired degree of doneness.

**Broil** by placing meat on rack of broiler pan 2 to 5 inches from heat. Broil under direct heat until top side is brown and meat is slightly more than ½ done. Turn and brown other side to desired degree of doneness. Season if desired.

**Broil** by placing meat in a heavy skillet or on a griddle. Do not add fat except for very lean cuts; brush pan with small amount of shorten-ing. Do not add water and do not cover. Cook slowly, turning occasionally and pouring off fat as it accumulates, until meat is brown on both sides and cooked to desired degree of doneness. Season if desired.

**Panfry** by browning meat on both sides in small amount of fat. Then season meat with salt and pepper, if desired, or add seasoning to ingredients for coating meat. Do not cover. Cook over medium heat, turning occasionally, to desired degree of doneness.

**Braise** less-tender cuts of meat. Brown meat slowly on both sides in heavy pan; pour off drippings. Season meat with salt, pepper, herbs or spices. Add small amount of liquid, such as water, bouillon or vegetable juice; cov-er tightly. Simmer on top of range or in 300°F to 325°F oven until tender.

**Cook in liquid** the large, less tender cuts of meat and meats to be used in stews and soups. Brown meat on all sides if desired. Cover with water, bouillon or tomato juice to assure uni-form cooking without turning. Cover pan tightly; simmer until tender but do not boil. If making stew or soup, add vegetables to the meat just long enough to cook before serving.

# How to Cut and Cook Large (Beef-in-a-Bag) Cuts of Meat

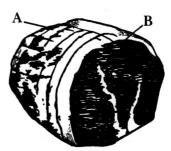

**Boneless Beef Chuck Roll** can be cut into roasts, steaks and cubes. It can be cut into as many roasts of whatever size you wish. Steaks intended for braising should be cut from the center portion. For best results, slice steaks no thinner than 1 inch. Leave netting or strings intact during cutting and cooking both roasts and steaks. To cook a roast section that has been cut into halves, tie strings to retain shape. Any part of the chuck roll can be cut into cubes or used for ground beef.

**Boneless Beef Tip (cap off)** can be cut into roasts, steaks and cubes. With round surface of beef up, cut with the grain into halves from A to B. Use the solid half (it holds together better) as a roast or cut it across the grain into steaks (¾ to 1 inch thick for braising, ½ inch thick for panfrying). Use other half (loose side) as a roast. Tie strings to help retain shape of beef during cooking. The loose half or tapered end of the other half also can be cut into cubes.

| Cooking Method | |
|---|---|
| Roasts | braise |
| Steaks | braise, marinate, broil |
| Cubes | braise, cook in liquid |

| Cooking Method | |
|---|---|
| Roasts | roast |
| Steaks | braise, panfry |
| Cubes | braise, cook in liquid |

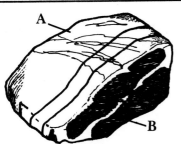

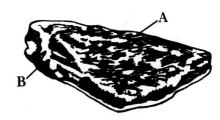

**Boneless Beef Top Sirloin (Butt)** can be cut into steaks and roasts. With fat side of beef up, slice into steaks across the grain (1 to 2 inches thick for broiling, 1 inch thick or less for pan-broiling or panfrying). Top sirloin also can be cut into halves from A to B for roasts or cut into halves and sliced across the grain for smaller steaks.

**Boneless Beef Brisket** can be cut into roasts. With fat side of beef down, use knife to separate the 2 muscle sections, removing the flat cut A from the muscle underneath B. Cut from tip of the flat cut as close to underside of A as possible. As the flat cut separates, pull steadily on it to aid separation. Remove flat cut and cut it into 2 roasts. Trim fat around the point as desired.

| Cooking Method | |
|---|---|
| Steaks | broil, panfry, panbroil |
| Roasts | roast |

| Cooking Method | |
|---|---|
| Braise | cook in liquid |

We are indebted to the Beef Industry Council of the National Livestock and Meat Board for cutting instructions for Beef-in-a-Bag and other materials.

# Carving Meats
## How to Carve Beef

**Blade Pot Roast:** Place roast on carving board or platter. Insert fork in meat; cut between muscles and around bones (bones are easily removed). Remove in solid sections, one at a time. Place each section with meat grain parallel to board. Carve across grain of meat into ¼-inch slices

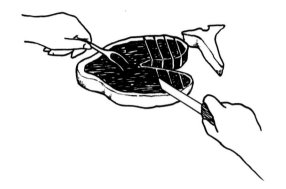

**Porterhouse Steak:** Place steak on carving board or platter with bone facing carver's right (or to the left if left-handed). Insert fork in steak; cut closely around bone. Set bone aside. Holding meat with fork, carve 1-inch wide slices across full width of steak. For thick steaks, slice meat on the diagonal (see Corned Beef Brisket instructions).

**Brisket:** Place brisket on carving board or platter. Carve across faces of brisket as shown. Make slices in rotation so that faces are equal in size. Cut thin slices at a slight angle, always across the grain.

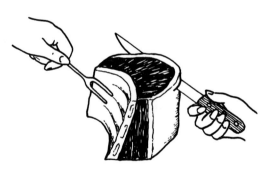

**Standing Rib Roast:** Place roast with large side down on carving board or platter. If necessary, remove a wedge-shaped slice from bottom so roast will be stable. Allow roast to stand 15 to 20 minutes for easier carving. To carve, insert fork on rib side just below first rib. Slice from outside of roast toward rib side. After making several slices, cut along inner side of rib bone with knife. As each slice is released, slide knife under it and lift to plate.

## How to Carve Lamb

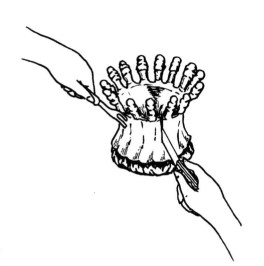

**Crown Roast:** Place roast on carving board or platter. Remove any garnish that may impede carving from center of crown. Slice down between the ribs, lifting out 1 rib at a time. Using spoon, serve stuffing from center of crown. The average crown roast contains about 14 ribs, but large crowns with 40 to 50 ribs can be specially ordered. To make carving and serving easier, the backbone should be completely removed at the market.

**Leg of Lamb:** Place roast on carving board or platter with the shank bone to carver's right (or to left if left-handed). Cut a few lengthwise slices from the thin side. Turn the leg over so that it rests firmly on the cut side. Make vertical slices to the leg bone, then cut horizontally along bone to release slices.

## How to Carve Pork

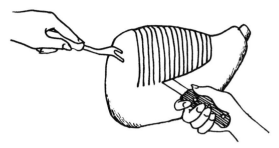

**Whole Ham:** Place ham on carving board or platter with the shank bone to right. Cut a few slices from the thin side (thin side will face toward carver if ham is a left leg, away from carver if ham is a right leg). Rest ham firmly on cut side. Make slices down to bone. Make horizontal cut along bone to release slices.

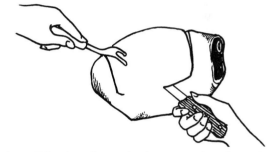

**Arm Picnic:** Place picnic on carving board or platter. Cut off a lengthwise slice from underside of picnic. Rest meat firmly on cut surface. Make vertical cuts as shown; turn knife and cut horizontally along bone to remove boneless piece to another surface for slicing. For more servings, cut remaining meat from arm bone and slice.

**Loin Roast:** Place roast on carving board or platter. Remove backbone for easy carving. Place roast with the rib side facing carver. Insert fork in roast; cut slices on each side of rib bones (every other slice will contain a bone).

# Nuts

A nut is actually a dry fruit that has an edible kernel enclosed in a woody shell. Fresh
nuts feel heavy for their size and do not rattle in the shells; fresh shelled
nuts are plump and fairly uniform in color and size — not dark or shriveled. Chopped nuts
are usually a better bargain than whole nuts or halves. (See also Yields
and Equivalents, page 133 and Storing Foods, pages 152 and 154)

**Almonds**, the largest tree crop from California, are widely available whole (blanched or unblanched), chopped, sliced or slivered. Sweet (unseasoned) almonds are used in baking and candy or are ground into paste for use in cakes, cookies and other bakings. Although bitter almonds are not eaten raw, the oils from them are used in almond flavoring.

**Cashews** are kidney-shaped nuts from the tropics. They are eaten roasted and salted as cocktail or dessert nuts. Cashews are used in baking, in cashew butter and in Chinese cooking, particularly chicken dishes.

**Black walnuts**, which are native to the United States, are larger than the more common European walnuts and have a thicker, harder shell and a unique flavor. They are used in candies, cakes and ice cream.

**Chestnuts**, chiefly imported from Italy, are available from September to March. Fresh chestnuts have smooth, shiny shells that feel heavy for their size. Chestnuts are boiled, roasted or preserved in sugar syrup for eating and also are used in stews, soups, stuffings, desserts or combined with vegetables.

**Brazil** nuts, from Brazil, are large with heavy, creamy kernels and a higher fat content than most nuts. They are available all year but may be best in the winter. They are used whole or sliced in candies and fruitcakes.

**Filberts**, also known as hazelnuts, are grown chiefly in Europe — some are grown domestically. Filberts in the shell that feel heavy have fuller kernels.

**Macadamia** nuts, from Hawaii, California, Florida and Australia, have a sweet, slightly salty flavor and are crisp and oily. Because the shell is so hard, the nuts are sold shelled, roasted and salted. They are used as cocktail nuts and chopped for dessert toppings.

**Pine** nuts are small seeds from a variety of pine trees grown in the southern United States, Mexico and the Mediterranean area of Europe. They are available shelled and in the shells, are tender and have a sweet, mild flavor. Pine nuts are used in pasta sauces, pastries, salads, other sauces and vegetable dishes.

**Peanuts** are native to South America but grown in the United States. They are seeds from the pods of a vine of the pea family and are really legumes, not nuts. Peanuts are used as meat extenders in main dishes, toppings for salads, in candy and desserts.

**Pistachio** nuts are the seeds of the fruit of the pistachio evergreen tree grown in the Middle East and in California. The shells of the pistachio nut are half-open and grayish white in color in their natural state but are often dyed red. Pistachios are eaten as cocktail or dessert nuts and are also used for baking and in candies, desserts and ice cream.

**Pecans**, which are native to North America, are available all year but are in largest supply from September to November. They are available as whole nuts in the shell and as halves, pieces and meal. Pecans are used in stuffings, sprinkled on salads or vegetables and seasoned for snacks.

**Walnuts**, sometimes called English or Persian walnuts, are grown primarily in California. They are available in the shell, shelled and in halves or pieces. Walnuts are the most popular nut for cooking and are used for baking and in candies, ice cream, salads and stuffings.

## Problems and Solutions

☐ *How can I blanch almonds?*

Drop shelled nuts into boiling water. Remove from heat. Let stand until skins are loosened, 2 to 5 minutes. Pour off hot water; cover with cold water. Pinch each nut between thumb and finger to push off skins; spread nuts on plate to dry.

☐ *How do I slice or sliver almonds?*

Slice almonds by cutting blanched nuts crosswise into very thin slices with a sharp knife. Sliver almonds by cutting blanched nuts lengthwise into pieces that are match size in diameter. Almonds are easier to slice or sliver if they are cut when still moist and warm.

☐ *How do I toast slivered or sliced almonds?*

Spread slivered or sliced almonds in a shallow pan and cook uncovered in a 350°F oven, stirring frequently, until delicately browned, 6 to 10 minutes. Watch carefully to avoid burning. Toasting almonds enhances their flavor.

☐ *How many cups of nuts are in one pound?*

See Yields and Equivalents, page 133.

☐ *What is the best way to store nuts to keep them fresh?*

Shelled nuts will remain fresh for several months if stored tightly covered in the refrigerator. Freezing or refrigerating unopened cans of nuts will keep them fresh for a longer time. For both freshness and convenience, try chopping nuts and freezing them in measured packets, all ready to add to your favorite nut bread, pecan pie or candy.

☐ *How do I peel chestnuts?*

**Cut** a shallow crisscross on the side of each chestnut with the tip of a sharp, pointed knife.

**Add** enough water to cover chestnuts. Cover and simmer about 10 minutes; drain. While chestnuts are still warm, peel off outer shell and inner skin.

☐ *How do I roast chestnuts?*

Chestnuts are traditionally roasted over an open fire in the fireplace. The husk of the chestnut must be pierced before roasting to prevent the nut from exploding. A special pan with holes in the bottom is used to contain the nuts over the fire. Roasting is done over a hot fire in a few minutes. Chestnuts are eaten hot and served with salt.

# Pasta

Pasta is a generic Italian word describing pastes or doughs of ground wheat and water made in a vast variety of shapes and sizes. You can make pasta at home by hand or with a pasta maker and vary the flavor and color with whole wheat flour or spinach. The fresh pasta can be cooked immediately after preparation or dried and stored. Commercially prepared and dried Italian pasta is available in many varieties, along with American, German, Oriental, Jewish, Polish and Russian pastas. The cost of a pasta dish and its calorie content are primarily dependent on the added ingredients. (See also Storing Foods, page 148)

**Macaroni** is usually shaped like a hollow tube and may range from large to small, be straight or curved, shell shaped or in very tiny pieces for soups.

**Noodles** are flat, ribbonlike strips cut in narrow, medium and broad widths. American-style noodles contain egg; some Oriental-style noodles are made without egg.

**Spaghetti** is long or short rods of pasta.

| Pasta Yields | | |
|---|---|---|
| Uncooked | Cooked | Servings |
| Macaroni 6 or 7 ounces (2 cups) | 4 cups | 4 to 6 |
| Spaghetti 7 or 8 ounces | 4 cups | 4 to 6 |
| Egg Noodles 8 ounces (4 to 5 cups) | 4 to 5 cups | 4 to 6 |

## Problems and Solutions

□ *How do I measure uncooked spaghetti?*

Weigh spaghetti on a scale or estimate that a tightly held bundle the diameter of a quarter will weigh about four ounces (depending on length) and will make about two servings.

□ *Can pasta be used interchangeably?*

All cooked pasta can be used interchangeably, measure for measure, in recipes. In recipes calling for a given measure of uncooked pasta, substitution may be difficult because of variations in weight.

□ *How can I tell when pasta is done?*

Cook pasta the minimum number of minutes directed on the package; then test it by cutting several strands with fork against side of kettle. Most people prefer pasta that is firm (al dente) to the bite rather than soft and mushy.

□ *Should I rinse pasta after cooking?*

No, pasta is usually best when cooked just before it is to be served or combined with other ingredients. If pasta is to be used in a cold salad, rinse in cold water; to prevent sticking together, add salad dressing while pasta is still warm, then refrigerate.

□ *How can I prevent water from boiling over when I cook pasta?*

Add 2 tablespoons cooking oil to the water.

## Pasta Identification by Shape

The many varieties of pasta on the market offer a fascinating assortment of sizes and shapes. Some shapes are known by more than one name. You can often determine size of pasta from the Italian suffix — "oni" means the pasta is large, and "elle," "ina," "ini," and "iti," mean the pasta is small.

### Pasta Description and Use

| Specific Name | Shape | Description | Use |
|---|---|---|---|
| **Macaroni** | | | |
| Alphabets | | tiny pasta alphabet | soups |
| Anelli | | tiny pasta rings | soups |
| Conchiglie | | smooth or ridged shell-shaped pasta in several sizes | soups or stuffed |
| Ditali | | large pasta "thimbles" with ridges | casseroles, salads, soups or with sauces |
| Elbow macaroni | | curved tubes in a variety of sizes and lengths | casseroles, soups |
| Farfalle | | pasta shaped like bows in a variety of sizes and colors | soups, stuffings |
| Lumache | | small to medium size snail-shaped pasta | casseroles, salads or with sauces |
| Macaroni | | pasta tubes in a variety of sizes and shapes | casseroles or soups |
| Mostaccioli | | medium-sized pasta tubes with diagonally cut ends | served with hearty meat or tomato sauce |
| Orzo | | tiny pasta resembling oats | soups or cooked like rice |
| Rigatoni | | slightly curved small tubes | casseroles or soups |
| Risini | | tiny rice-shaped pasta | soups |
| Ziti | | short, smooth tubes | casseroles |
| **Noodles** | | | |
| Fettuccini | | about ¼-inch-wide ribbon noodles, straight or in coils | buttered or in rich meat sauce |
| Lasagne | | wide pasta, sometimes with curly edges | baked dishes |
| Noodle flakes | | very fine egg pasta sheets cut into ¼-inch squares | soups |

## Pasta Description and Use

| Specific Name | Shape | Description | Use |
|---|---|---|---|
| Tagliatelle | | ¾-inch-wide egg noodles | casseroles or with sauces |
| **Spaghetti** | | | |
| Bucatini | | typical spaghetti but hollow instead of solid | with sauces |
| Capellini | | thin, often coiled spaghetti | with sauces |
| Fusilli | | strands of spiral-shaped pasta | with sauces |
| Linguine | | flat, narrow, long | casseroles or with sauces |
| Spaghettini | | long, fine-cut strands of spaghetti | with sauces |
| Vermicelli | | straight or folded strands of very thin spaghetti | with sauces |
| **Miscellaneous Pasta** | | | |
| Cannelloni | | 4- to 6-inch pieces of large, fresh pasta rolled around a filling | baked with sauces |
| Manicotti | | large smooth or ridged pasta tubes | cooked, filled with cheese or meat and baked |
| Ravioli | | pasta dumpling filled with spinach and ricotta cheese or meat and herbs | served with sauce |
| Won ton skins | | thin soft squares of noodle dough wrapped around or folded over filling of meat, vegetables or seafood | deep-fried, boiled or steamed |
| **Other** | | | |
| Cellophane noodles | | hard, clear white noodles made from mung peas; turn translucent when cooked in liquid, puffy and crisp when deep-fat fried | Oriental-style dishes |
| Rice sticks | | thin, brittle white noodles made from rice powder | softened in liquid, then stir-fried or deep-fat fried in Oriental-style dishes |

# Pastry & Pies

The secrets of pastry making are many but really simple to learn. As with any skill, practice makes perfect. From green apple pie served warm from the oven to chilled, glazed, fresh strawberry pie, the accomplished cook can build a repertoire of pies for all tastes. So here are the secrets of making flaky pastry, lofty meringues, beautiful edgings and delicious fillings, not to mention answers to troublesome questions about rolling out pie crust and preventing shrinkage during baking.

## Problems and Solutions

☐ *What are some of the qualities of a good pie crust?*

A good pie crust is of even thickness and has a rough surface with small blisters. It is delicate light brown in color, dry but tender, crisp, light and flaky in texture and has a rich pleasing flavor.

☐ *Can I use self-rising flour in my pie crust?*

Yes, self-rising flour can be used for making pie crust, but because this flour contains salt, omit any additional salt. Pastry made with self-rising flour will have a slightly different character — mealy and tender rather than flaky and tender.

☐ *Can I use lard if the recipe for pie crust calls for shortening?*

Lard can be used in place of shortening, but the amount should be reduced because lard has more shortening power than hydrogenated shortening. If a one-crust recipe calls for ⅓ cup plus 1 tablespoon shortening, use ⅓ cup lard. If a two-crust recipe calls for ½ cup plus 2 tablespoons shortening, use ½ cup lard.

☐ *What kind of pie plate should I use?*

Heat-resistant glass plates give the flakiest results, but aluminum pans with a dull finish or darkened pans yield a well-baked, tender, browned undercrust in pies. Shiny metal pans reflect the heat and result in soggy, soaked undercrusts. Use the pan size recommended in the recipe.

☐ *How can I prevent pastry from sticking to the rolling surface and rolling pin?*

Use a pastry cloth, into which flour has been rubbed, and a stockinet-covered rolling pin to prevent pastry from sticking during rolling. Run rolling pin across the floured board to lightly coat it with flour before rolling.

□ *How can I roll pastry into a uniform circle instead of a lopsided one?*

**Roll** pastry from center to outside edge in four directions, giving a quarter turn occasionally to keep pastry even as you roll. For even thickness, lift rolling pin as you approach the edge.

**Keep pastry circular** by occasionally pushing ragged edges in gently with cupped hands.

**If edges begin to break**, pinch together at once and continue rolling.

# One Crust Pies

For a one-crust pie in a baked shell, the pastry is pricked and baked separately, then a cooked or uncooked filling is poured into the baked shell. These pies include cream, fresh uncooked fruit, meringue-topped, refrigerated and frozen, tarts and pies in special crusts. For a one-crust pie baked in pastry, the pastry is not pricked. If it were, the filling would seep under the crust during baking. These pies include custard, pecan and pumpkin.

## Problems and Solutions

□ *How can I prevent a baked pie shell from shrinking in the pie plate?*

Roll pastry two inches beyond the edge of the inverted pie plate. Ease the pastry gently into the plate, pressing toward the center with fingertips, then toward the edge of the plate to remove any air bubbles. Doing this keeps the pastry from stretching, which causes shrinking during baking. Trim overhanging edge of pastry one inch from rim of plate. Fold and roll pastry under, even with plate. Flute as desired, then hook fluted edge over rim of pie plate to secure it.

□ *What will prevent my baked pie shell from puffing up as it bakes?*

Prick pastry thoroughly to prevent puffing during baking. Bake pie shell as directed in recipe. Dried beans are sometimes used for this purpose, too. After pricking the fluted pastry, but before baking it, gently press lightweight aluminum foil into the pastry-lined plate. Fill with dried beans (about 4 cups for a 9-inch pie plate); bake as directed in recipe, except — remove liner and beans a few minutes before end of baking period.

☐ *What is the secret of attractive fluted edges around a baked pie shell?*

**Fork edge:** Flatten pastry evenly on rim of pie plate, and trim even with edge of plate. Press firmly around edge with tines of fork, dipping fork into flour occasionally to prevent sticking.

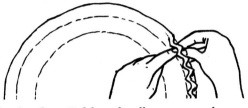

**Pinch edge:** Fold and roll pastry under, even with plate to form an even pastry rim. Place index finger on inside of pastry rim, thumb and index finger on outside. Pinch pastry into V-shape, repeating along entire edge. Pinch again to sharpen V's.

**Rope edge:** Fold and roll pastry under, even with plate to form pastry rim. Place thumb on pastry rim at an angle. Pinch pastry by pressing knuckle down into pastry toward thumb. Repeat along entire edge.

**Ruffle edge:** Fold and roll pastry under, even with plate to form pastry rim. Place thumb and index finger about one inch apart on pastry rim. With other index finger, pull pastry toward outside. Repeat along entire edge.

☐ *How do you make tart shells?*

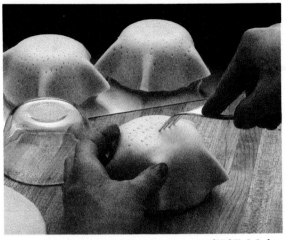

**Custard cup tarts:** Heat oven to 475°F. Make pastry for 8-inch one-crust pie and divide the dough into 4 equal 3½-inch parts. Roll each into a 6-inch circle. Turn custard cups upside down. Fit rounds of dough over outside of custard cups and prick well with a fork. Place pastry-covered cups on cookie sheet and bake 8 to 10 minutes. Carefully remove tart shells from cups when cool.

**Foil cup tarts:** Heat oven to 475°F. Make pastry for 8-inch one-crust pie and roll pastry to cover 12 × 8-inch piece of heavy foil. Mark six 4-inch squares with knife. Cut through dough and foil with scissors; prick dough well with a fork. Turn sides of dough and foil up 1 inch. Pinch corners of foil and pastry to shape tarts. Place on cookie sheet and bake 12 to 15 minutes. Cool; remove foil from tarts.

☐ *What are the characteristics of a good cream pie filling?*

A good cream pie filling is smooth in texture and tends to hold its shape when cut. It has a pleasing flavor with no raw, starchy taste.

☐ *How should I store custard or cream pies after baking?*

Refrigerate cream and custard pies promptly; they should never be allowed to stand at room temperature because there is a possibility of salmonella (a food spoilage bacteria) developing in foods that contain eggs and milk.

□ *Can I freeze pie shells?*

Yes, freeze pie shells unbaked or baked. Frozen baked shells will keep four months, unbaked shells two months. To thaw baked pie shells, unwrap and let stand at room temperature or heat in 350°F oven about 6 minutes. Do not thaw unbaked shells; bake immediately after removal from freezer.

□ *Can I freeze cream pies?*

No, cream, custard and meringue-topped pies do not freeze well. The cream and custard fillings separate and the meringues toughen and shrink.

□ *How can I avoid lumpy cream fillings?*

The egg yolks in cream fillings must be added to the hot mixture very slowly to avoid lumping. Gradually stir at least half of the hot mixture (milk, sugar and cornstarch) into the slightly beaten egg yolks. Blend this mixture back into the remaining hot mixture; boil and stir 1 minute. Follow recipe directions.

□ *How can I increase the volume of a meringue topping for a pie?*

For best volume, use egg whites that have been brought to room temperature, but separate eggs first when they are cold. Be sure bowl and beaters are free from grease and that egg whites contain no particles of egg yolk; grease or yolk prevent egg whites from beating up. Beat in the sugar gradually and continue beating until it is completely dissolved. Test by rubbing a bit of meringue between fingers or tasting to make sure it is smooth, not grainy. Swirl or pull up points of meringue after piling onto pie filling.

□ *My meringue shrinks away from the crust after baking; what can I do?*

Pile meringue onto hot pie filling, carefully sealing the meringue to crust all around edge of pie. This technique will help to prevent shrinking and "weeping." After baking, cool pie gradually at room temperature to prevent shrinkage of meringue.

□ *What can I do to keep my graham cracker crust from crumbling after it is baked?*

Press the mixture of crumbs, sugar and butter firmly against bottom and side of pie plate. Press another pie plate of the same diameter firmly into the crumb crust to make it firm and smooth. Remove second pie plate and bake crust as directed.

# Two Crust Pies

Two-crust pies include a wide variety of fruit fillings from apples to strawberries. Dumplings, which are whole, halved or sliced fruit wrapped in pie crust, can be considered a kind of two-crust pie. Turnovers are individual pies made from pastry that is filled with fruit, folded and baked or fried in deep fat.

## Problems and Solutions

□ *What are the steps in preparation of a two-crust pie?*

The bottom pastry for a two-crust pie is not pricked with a fork. (The filling prevents air bubbles from forming in the crust.) With scissors, snip overhanging edge of bottom pastry evenly ½ inch from rim of pie plate; add fruit as recipe directs. Roll out top crust two inches beyond edge of pie plate; trim to an even circle. Fold into fourths; cut slits to allow steam to escape. Carefully place folded pastry evenly on top of filling. Unfold, leaving a one-inch rim of pastry beyond edge of plate. Fold and roll pastry under edge of bottom pastry. Pinch edges gently with fingers to seal. Flute edge (see page 94). Bake as recipe directs.

□ *What are the characteristics of a good fruit filling?*

Fruit pieces should retain a fresh, natural color and be tender but hold their shape after baking. The fruit filling should tend to hold its shape when lukewarm or cold but will run out onto the plate when pie is cut. The fruit should have a pleasing flavor with no starchy taste.

□ *How can I make special occasion designs on the top crust of a pie?*

Roll pastry for top crust, but do not cut slits. With small cookie cutter or pattern, cut out design from center of crust. Examples are a heart for Valentine's Day, a hatchet for President's Day, a shamrock for St. Patrick's Day, a rabbit for Easter, a flag for Fourth of July, a cat or pumpkin for Halloween, a turkey for Thanksgiving and a tree for Christmas.

□ *How can I give a special finished look to the top crust of my pie?*

**Glazed crust:** Brush crust with beaten egg or egg yolk mixed with a little water before baking.

**Shiny crust:** Brush the crust lightly with milk before baking.

**Sugary crust:** Using your fingers or a pastry brush, moisten crust lightly with water, then sprinkle lightly with sugar before baking.

☐ *How can I make fancy lattice crust tops on my pies?*

**Lattice Top** (1): Roll circle for top crust and cut circle into strips about ½ inch wide. Use a sharp knife or a pastry wheel for more decorative strips. Place five to seven strips (depending on size of pie) across filling in pie plate. Weave a cross strip through center by first folding back every other strip halfway and placing a strip across the strips that remain unfolded. Unfold the strips and fold back the alternates. Weave in another strip. Continue weaving until lattice is complete. Trim ends of strips and fold edge of lower crust over them, building up a high edge. Seal and flute edge.

**Diamond Top** (2): Follow the same procedure as for lattice top except weave or lay second half of pastry strips diagonally across first strips on filling. Fold trimmed edge of bottom crust over strips and flute edge of pie.

**Twister Top** (3): Twist and place five to seven strips across filling in pie plate. Twist the same number of strips and place in the opposite direction, making a lattice top (not woven) or a diamond top (place strips diagonally on filling). Fold trimmed edge of bottom crust over strips and flute edge of pie.

**Spiral Top** (4): Beginning from center of pie, twist one strip and place in spiral on pie, adding length by moistening ends of other strips and pinching. Moisten trimmed edge of bottom crust; place tightly twisted pastry strip around edge, pressing to seal.

☐ *Can I freeze two-crust pies?*

Yes, freeze baked pies first to make wrapping easier, then wrap with freezer wrap or place in freezer plastic bags, seal and label. Pies are baked before freezing to prevent soggy crusts. Baked frozen pies will keep up to four months.

☐ *How do I heat frozen baked pies?*

Unwrap frozen two-crust pie and thaw at room temperature 1 hour. Heat in 375°F oven on lowest rack for 35 to 40 minutes until warm.

☐ *Why do two-crust pies sometimes have soggy bottoms?*

The secret of a well-baked tender undercrust is in choosing the right pie plate or pan and baking long enough at a high temperature — usually 425°F. Refer to page 92 for the correct pie plate to use.

☐ *How can I prevent the edge of my pie from browning too much during baking?*

To prevent excessive browning, cover edge with a two- to three-inch strip of aluminum foil and mold to edge of pie. Bake as recipe directs. Remove foil fifteen minutes before end of baking time to allow edge to brown.

☐ *If I want to freeze pies in aluminum foil pie pans, how should I bake them for a brown bottom crust?*

Place pies in aluminum foil pans on a cookie sheet so the bottom crust will brown evenly. Foil pans are shiny and reflect heat, the cookie sheet helps to trap heat next to the pie.

# Poultry

Poultry, whether versatile chicken and turkey or elegant cornish hen and pheasant, adds great variety to menus. Cook it simply or with special ingredients to create a recipe all your own. Read the guide below for a brief description of each cooking method, then read on to learn the secrets of using herbs, wine, broth or seasonings to make poultry a specialty of your house. (See also Storing Foods, pages 151 and 154)

## How to Select and Cook Poultry

| Type | Weight | Retail Cut | Cooking Method |
|---|---|---|---|
| **Chicken,** | | | |
| broiler-fryer | 2 to 3½ pounds | whole | roast, cook in liquid |
| | | halves | bake, broil, braise, grill |
| | | quarters | bake, broil, panfry, grill |
| | | pieces | bake, broil, panfry, cook in liquid, grill |
| capon | 4 to 7 pounds | whole | roast |
| roaster | 3½ to 6 pounds | whole | roast, cook in liquid |
| stewing | 4½ to 6 pounds | whole | cook in liquid |
| **Chicken Parts,** | | | |
| breast | 12 to 15 ounces | whole or split | bake, broil, panfry, grill |
| boned breast | about 4 ounces | split | bake, broil, panfry, grill |
| thigh | 4 ounces | whole | bake, broil, panfry, grill |
| drumstick | 4 to 5 ounces | whole | bake, broil, panfry, grill |
| giblets | 3 to 4 ounces | heart, gizzard, liver | braise, cook in liquid broil, panfry |
| wing | about 2 ounces | whole | bake, braise, panfry, cook in liquid, grill |
| **Cornish Hen** | 1½ pounds or less | whole | roast, broil, grill |
| **Duckling** | 4 to 5 pounds | whole | roast |
| **Goose, domestic** | 7 to 13 pounds | whole | roast |
| **Turkey** | 5 to 24 pounds | whole | roast |
| **Turkey Parts,** | | | |
| boneless roll | 3 to 9 pounds | whole | roast |
| breast | about 5 pounds | whole | roast, poach, grill |
| drumstick | about 1 pound | whole | poach, cook in liquid, grill |
| hindquarter (drumstick and thigh) | about 4 pounds | whole | roast, poach, cook in liquid |
| quarter/half | 5 to 12 pounds | whole | roast, poach, grill |
| wing | about 12 ounces | whole | cook in liquid |

| How to Select and Cook Wild Game | | | |
|---|---|---|---|
| Type | Weight | Retail Cut | Cooking Method |
| **Game, Wild** | | | |
| duck | 1½ to 2 pounds | whole | roast |
| pheasant | 2 to 3 pounds | whole | roast, braise |
| quail | 3 to 5 ounces | whole | roast, braise |

# General Cooking Methods

**Roast** chicken by placing breast side up and wings folded across back with tips touching on rack in shallow roasting pan. Brush with shortening, oil, margarine or butter. Do not add water; do not cover. Roast at temperature given in recipe.

Place a tent of aluminum foil loosely over turkey when it begins to turn golden. When ⅔ done, cut band of skin or string holding legs.

**Broil** young chickens weighing 2½ pounds or less by placing chicken halves, quarters or pieces skin sides down on rack in broiler pan; brush with melted margarine or butter. For halves or quarters, turn wing tips onto back side. Place broiler pan so top of chicken is 7 to 9 inches from heat. Broil, turning once and brushing with margarine or butter, until chicken is done, 50 to 60 minutes.

**Grill** on charcoal, gas or electric grill according to manufacturer's directions until poultry is done.

**Panfry** chicken pieces by browning on all sides in small amount of fat; reduce heat. Cover tightly and simmer, turning once or twice, until thickest pieces are done, 30 to 40 minutes. Remove cover during last 5 minutes of cooking to crisp chicken.

**Braise** chicken or game by browning pieces slowly on all sides in heavy pan; pour off drippings. Add small amount of liquid, such as water, bouillon or wine; cover tightly. Simmer on top of range or in 325°F oven until thickest pieces of poultry are done, 35 to 60 minutes.

**Poach** chicken or turkey pieces by cooking in enough water to cover bottom of pan. Sprinkle with salt and pepper and heat to boiling. Reduce heat. Cover and simmer until done.

**Cooking in liquid** is appropriate for stewing hens, turkey hindquarters, chicken wings and gizzards. Whole chickens can be cooked in liquid for use in salads, casseroles or creamed dishes. Place chicken in kettle with just enough water to cover. Add salt, pepper or herbs if desired. Heat to boiling; reduce heat. Cover and simmer until thickest pieces are done.

## Problems and Solutions

☐ *How many cups of cooked poultry can you get from different birds?*

| Type and Ready-to-Cook Weight | Approximate Cooked Yield |
|---|---|
| 3- to 4-pound broiler-fryer chicken | 3 to 4 cups |
| 4½- to 6-pound stewing chicken | 4½ to 6 cups |
| 5- to 6-pound boneless turkey roll | 10 to 12 cups |
| 12-pound turkey | 14 cups |

☐ *How much stuffing should I put in different size birds?*

| Type | Bread Stuffing |
|---|---|
| Chicken | ¾ cup per pound |
| Cornish hen | 1 cup per hen |
| Turkey | ¾ cup per pound |

Prepare stuffing and stuff poultry lightly just before roasting — not ahead of time. Remove all stuffing from cooked poultry after serving; refrigerate in covered container and use within three days. Stuffing also can be wrapped and frozen for one month.

# Cutting Up a Chicken

If you have a preference for certain parts of a chicken, or when chicken parts are on special, it is false economy to buy a whole chicken. However, whole chickens are usually less expensive than cut-up chickens, so here is the way you can cut the chicken into parts. Poultry freezes well and can be wrapped and frozen in quantities of parts just right for your family.

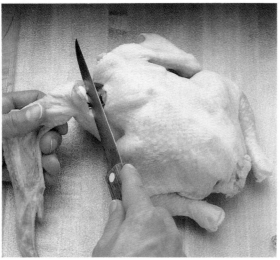

**1. Start** with a sharp knife. Cut off each wing by cutting wing joint, then rolling knife to let blade follow through at the curve of the joint.

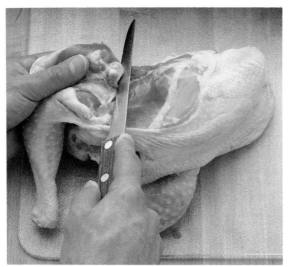

**2. Cut** off legs by cutting skin between leg and body; cut through the meat between tail and hip joint. Pull leg away to separate meat from bone, then cut through remaining skin.

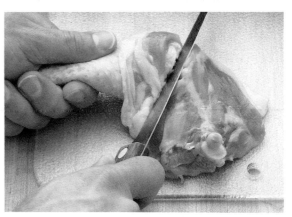

**3. Cut** drumsticks away from thighs by cutting ⅛ inch from thin fat line that runs crosswise at the joint between drumstick and thigh.

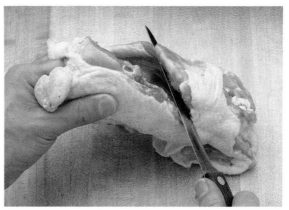

**4. Separate** backbone by holding the body with the neck end down and cutting along each side of the backbone through the rib joints.

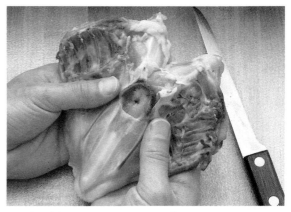

**5. Place** breast with skin side down and neck end away from you, then cut through cartilage at V of neck. Bend back both sides to pull and pop out the bone and cartilage. Pull out bone and cartilage. Cut breast into halves.

# Boning a Chicken Breast

Chicken breasts are light meat and the meatiest part of the bird. They are sold whole or split. Here's how you can remove the bones from breasts to be cooked whole, or halved and pounded thin into cutlets or cut into pieces for stir-frying.

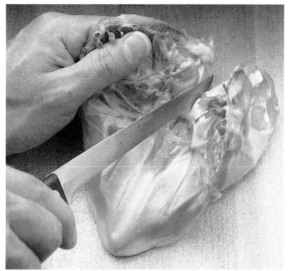

**1. Place** whole chicken breast, skin side down, on cutting surface. Cut through just the white gristle at the end of the keel bone (the dark bone at the center of the breast).

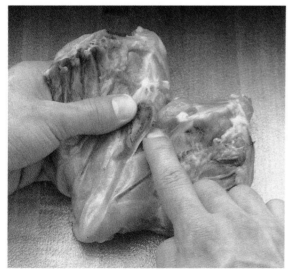

**2. Bend** breast halves back to pop out the keel bone. Loosen keel bone by running tip of index finger around both sides. Remove in one or two pieces.

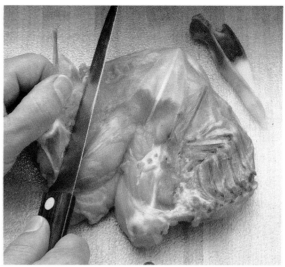

**3. Working** with 1 side of breast, cut rib cages away from breast, cutting through shoulder joint to remove entire rib cage. Repeat on other side.

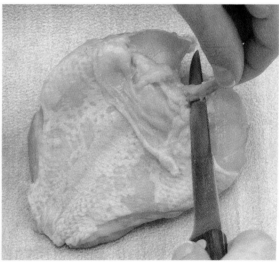

**4. Turn** chicken breast over and cut away wishbone. Slip knife under white tendons on either side of breast; loosen and pull tendons out. Remove skin if desired. To form cutlets, place chicken breast quarters between 2 pieces of waxed paper and pound thin with a mallet or rolling pin.

Or easier still, cook unboned chicken breasts in white wine, broth or water to which herbs and/or a little cut-up celery, carrots and onion have been added. While breasts are still warm, remove skin, bones and cartilage with your fingers. Chill meat before slicing.

# Carving Poultry and Game

Carving poultry efficiently into attractive servings requires a well-sharpened knife and a stable cutting surface, preferably a wooden board. An important aid to producing whole, smooth slices is to allow the cooked bird to rest at room temperature for approximately 20 minutes before carving.

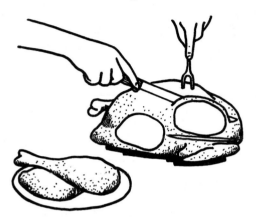

**Chicken:** Cut through joint between leg and body. Remove leg; cut between drumstick and thigh. Remove wing, cutting through joint between wing and body. Cut horizontally into breast just above wing. Insert fork in top of breast, and starting halfway up breast, carve thin slices down to the cut, working upward. Repeat carving procedure on opposite side.

**Goose:** Remove wings, cutting through joint between wing and body. Remove legs, cutting through joint between leg and body. (Cutting leg joint with a poultry shears may be easier than using a knife because the leg joint is farther back and harder to get at than on a chicken.) Cut away each of the 2 sections of breast meat in 1 piece. Slice the breast meat, thighs and drumsticks into smaller portions.

**Turkey:** Remove drumstick and thigh by pulling leg away from body and cutting through joint with knifepoint. Cut dark meat completely from body by following body contour while slicing with knife.

**Slice** dark meat from drumstick and thigh on separate plate. Cut through connecting joint between drumstick and thigh. Remove meat from drumstick by slicing at an angle.

**Slice** thigh by holding firmly on plate with fork and cutting even slices parallel to the bone.

**Cut** into breast, making horizontal cut just above wing and cutting all the way to the bone.

**Carve** breast by slicing downward to horizontal cut. Start each new slice slightly higher up on breast; keep slices thin and even.

# Rice

Rice, of which there are more than 7,000 varieties throughout the world, is the staple grain that feeds about half the world's population. Grown in Asia, Europe and America, the kinds of rice and their cooking methods vary from country to country. Success in preparing a simple bowl of steaming white rice or a spicy brown rice pilaf depends on choosing the kind of rice and cooking method that best suits your family's taste.

**Brown** (1) rice is whole grained and unpolished with both the hull and a small amount of the bran removed. Brown rice has a slightly chewy texture and a nutty flavor.

**Converted** (2) rice, also called parboiled or processed rice, is treated before milling to force the vitamins and minerals from the hull, bran and germ into the starchy part of the grain before polishing. Parboiled rice cooks into separate, plump grains and has a bland flavor.

**Precooked** (3) or instant rice is long grain white rice which has been commercially cooked, rinsed and dried before packaging. Precooked rice is dry and tender with a bland flavor. When cooked, its grains do not separate as fully as those of parboiled rice.

**Regular** (4) rice has been milled to remove the hull, germ and most of the bran. Regular white rice may have either long or short grains and has a tender texture and bland flavor.

**Wild** (5) rice is the seed of a grass that grows in shallow lakes and marshes. It is long grained, dark greenish brown in color and has a chewy texture and a distinctive flavor.

## Problems and Solutions

□ *How much cooked rice can I expect from 1 cup of raw rice?*

The yield of cooked rice varies with the kind of rice cooked because of the milling and treatment process used. Look for the yield on the package. The following chart gives approximate cooked yields for different kinds of rice.

| Rice Yields | | |
|---|---|---|
| Type of Rice | Uncooked Rice | Cooked Rice |
| Brown | 1 cup | 4 cups |
| Parboiled | 1 cup | 3 to 4 cups |
| Precooked | 1 cup | 2 cups |
| Regular | 1 cup | 3 cups |
| Wild | 1 cup | 3 cups |

□ *Should I rinse rice after cooking?*

No, rinsing rice after cooking causes some of the nutrients to be lost.

# Sauces

A velvety and perfectly seasoned sauce often "makes the dish," as French chefs say. Whether you plan to specialize in the classics like hollandaise or improvise with canned soups and packaged mixes, you should know your sauces.

**Canned sauces** come in the form of white sauce, hollandaise, tomato and also a wide assortment of soups, which can be diluted to make sauces. Vary white sauce by adding curry powder to make curry sauce. Change hollandaise into béarnaise-like sauce by adding minced onion, snipped fresh tarragon, chervil leaves and a little white wine. Make a creole sauce by adding chopped celery, green pepper, basil leaves, onion and red pepper sauce to tomato sauce.

**Dry sauce mixes** are sold in foil-lined packets in a variety of flavors and for many uses. Most dry mixes are completed by the addition of water or milk and a few minutes' cooking. Some call for the addition of sour cream or butter. Packet directions should be followed. Alternative uses for mixes in recipes are often printed on the packet.

## Recipe Sauces

**Espagnole sauce**, pictured (1) page 105, is a type of brown sauce because of its rich brown color and beef broth base. In addition, it contains white wine, thyme, bay leaf, carrot, onion, bacon and tomato purée.

## Problems and Solutions

□ *How can I intensify the color and flavor of my espagnole sauce?*

Add bottled browning sauce or reduce salt and add beef extract or instant bouillon to the sauce while cooking.

□ *How can I vary brown sauce?*

Make Bordelaise sauce by substituting red wine for half the beef broth and adding minced onion, snipped parsley, a bay leaf and a sprig of fresh thyme. Make mushroom sauce by adding sliced mushrooms (browned in margarine) and a few drops of Worcestershire.

**Hollandaise, (2)** page 105, is a cooked sauce thickened with egg and flavored with lemon juice. It is served hot with vegetables, poultry, fish and eggs.

## Problems and Solutions

□ *How can I prevent hollandaise from curdling during cooking?*

Cook hollandaise over very low heat; do not overcook. Be sure margarine melts slowly or is added slowly to give eggs time to cook and thicken the sauce without curdling.

□ *What should I do to restore curdled hollandaise to a smooth sauce?*

Add about 1 tablespoon boiling water to ¾ cup hollandaise and beat sauce vigorously with hand beater until smooth.

□ *How shall I store leftover hollandaise?*

Be sure to refrigerate leftover sauce immediately. It will keep several days. Before reheating, stir in about 1 teaspoon hot water for ¾ cup sauce. Cook and stir over low heat just until hot.

**Mayonnaise, (3)** page 105, is a thick sauce of oil and egg yolk in a permanent emulsion, seasoned with lemon juice or vinegar and seasonings. It is commonly used as a salad dressing or as a base for other sauce.

## Problem and Solution

□ *Can I make other sauces from mayonnaise?*

Make creamy onion dressing by mixing 2 parts mayonnaise with 1 part dairy sour cream and some finely chopped green onion. Make

dill sauce by mixing mayonnaise with snipped fresh dill; serve with seafood. Make Russian dressing by mixing 2 parts mayonnaise with 1 part chili sauce and a few drops of onion juice.

**Velouté sauce** can be made by heating melted margarine or butter with flour and adding chicken, veal or fish broth. It is similar to white sauce and is used with croquettes, eggs, poultry, seafood and meat dishes.

### Problem and Solution

□ *How can I vary velouté sauce?*

Make almond velouté sauce by adding toasted slivered almonds just before serving with veal or chicken. Make anchovy sauce by stirring anchovy paste into butter-flour mixture; use fish broth, omit salt and add snipped parsley.

**Vinaigrette,** (4) above, is a thin sauce, commonly called Classic French dressing, made from a combination of oil, vinegar, salt and pepper. It is served on salads and can be used as a marinade for vegetables, fish and meat.

### Problem and Solution

□ *How can I vary vinaigrette sauce?*

Make garlic vinaigrette by adding peeled garlic cloves; make Roquefort vinaigrette by adding crumbled Roquefort or bleu cheese; and make Lorenzo dressing by adding chili sauce to vinaigrette sauce.

**White sauce,** (5) above, can be thin, medium or thick in consistency and is the basis of a variety of sauces as well as a part of many recipes.

### Problems and Solutions

□ *How can I prevent my white sauce from scorching during cooking?*

Cook white sauce in a heavy, flat-bottomed pan over low heat, stirring constantly.

□ *How can I keep white sauce smooth?*

Cook white sauce over low heat, stirring constantly with a wooden spoon or wire whip. Remove from heat when stirring in milk; return to heat and continue cooking, stirring constantly, until thickened.

□ *If my white sauce does turn lumpy, what can I do?*

Strain lumpy white sauce through a wire sieve.

□ *How can I prevent a film from forming on white sauce after cooking?*

Place a circle of waxed paper or plastic wrap directly on surface of sauce to keep air from forming a film. If white sauce is made ahead of using, cool to room temperature, cover with waxed paper and refrigerate.

# Seafood-Fish

From the lordly lobster to the lowly panfish, versatile seafood and fish contribute a vast variety of flavors and textures to the table. They are a good source of protein and other nutrients, are generally low in fat and are quick cooking — virtues that suit them to today's more healthful life-style, with its emphasis on lighter eating, and less time for cooking. Whether simply broiled, baked or poached, fish can be served with a sauce or a topping of herbed butter and lemon juice. In combination with other foods, both seafood and fish are the basis of many classic recipes for soups, stews and chowders. They have a place in salads, casseroles and sandwiches as well. In seaboard regions of the United States and other nations, they are staples of the daily diet. (See also Shopping Secrets, page 146)

## Selecting and Cooking

Use the following chart to simplify selection and cooking methods for seafood and fish. Fish, like meat or poultry, can be fat or lean. Medium and high fat fish contain 5 to 15 percent fat, but certain species of lake trout, herring, mackerel and sardines can contain more than 15 percent fat. Lean fish contain less than 5 percent fat.

Drawn fish are whole but eviscerated. Dressed fish are eviscerated and scaled. They usually have head, tail and fins removed.

### How to Select and Cook Seafood and Fish

| Type of Seafood/Fish | Form Usually Purchased | Fat or Lean | General Cooking Method |
|---|---|---|---|
| Bass | whole, drawn, fillets | lean | bake, broil, panfry |
| Bluefish | whole, drawn, fillets | lean | bake, broil |
| Catfish | whole, dressed, skinned, steaks, fillets | fat | bake, broil, panfry |
| Clams | in the shell, shucked | lean | eat raw, bake, panfry, cook in liquid |
| Cod | drawn, dressed, steaks, fillets | lean | bake, barbecue, cook in liquid |
| Crab, dungeness, hard-shell, soft-shell | live, cooked | lean | cook in liquid |
| Crappie | whole, drawn, fillets | lean | broil, panfry |
| Croaker | whole, dressed, fillets | lean | broil, panfry |
| Flounder (others called sole: gray, lemon, rex) | whole, dressed, fillets | lean | bake, broil, panfry, poach |
| Grouper | whole, drawn, dressed, steaks, fillets | lean | bake, panfry, cook in liquid |

## How to Select and Cook Seafood and Fish

| Type of Seafood/Fish | Form Usually Purchased | Fat or Lean | General Cooking Method |
|---|---|---|---|
| Haddock | drawn, fillets | lean | bake, broil, panfry, poach |
| Hake | whole, drawn, dressed, fillets | lean | bake, broil, panfry, poach |
| Halibut | dressed, steaks | lean | bake, broil, panfry, poach |
| Herring, sea | whole | fat | bake, broil, panfry, pickle in brine, smoke |
| Lobster | live, cooked | lean | bake, cook in liquid |
| Mackerel | whole, drawn, fillets | fat | bake, broil, panfry, poach |
| Mullet | whole, fillets | lean | bake, broil, panfry, cook in liquid |
| Mussels | in the shell | lean | bake, panfry, cook in liquid |
| Oysters | in the shell, shucked | lean | eat raw, bake, panfry, poach, cook in liquid |
| Pike, northern, walleye | whole, dressed, fillets | lean | bake, broil, panfry |
| Pollock | drawn, dressed, steaks, fillets | lean | bake, broil, panfry, poach |
| Porgy (scup) | whole, dressed | lean | panfry |
| Red snapper | drawn, dressed, steaks, fillets | lean | bake, broil, panfry, poach |
| Rockfish | dressed, fillets | lean | bake, broil, panfry, poach |
| Salmon | drawn, dressed, steaks, fillets | fat | bake, broil, panfry, poach, smoke |
| Scallops | shucked | lean | bake, broil, panfry, poach |
| Sea bass | whole, dressed, fillets | lean | bake, broil, poach |
| Shad | whole, drawn, fillets | fat | bake, broil, panfry |
| Shrimp | headless in the shell, cooked | lean | bake, broil, panfry, cook in liquid |
| Smelt | whole, drawn | lean | deep fry, panfry |
| Sole, Dover | drawn, dressed, fillets | lean | bake, broil, panfry, poach |
| Tuna, albacore, bluefin, tunny, bonito | whole (if small), steaks | lean | bake, broil, poach |
| Trout, lake | drawn, dressed, fillets | fat | bake, broil, cook in liquid, smoke |
| Trout, sea (weakfish) | whole, drawn, dressed, fillets | lean | bake, broil, panfry |
| Whitefish | whole, drawn, dressed, fillets | fat | bake, poach |

# General Cooking Methods

Fresh seafood and freshwater fish can be cooked by dry heat (baking, broiling or cooking on a gas or charcoal grill) or by moist heat (poaching or cooking in liquid). They also can be panfried or deep fried. Dry heat methods are best for fat fish while moist heat, panfrying and deep frying are best for lean fish, allowing it to remain firm during cooking. Fish is fully cooked when the translucent flesh becomes opaque and flakes easily with a fork, but extended cooking toughens it and makes it dry. Whether fish comes from the market, frozen and thawed or just caught from the sea or a lake, these general cooking methods can be used.

**Bake** fish whole, stuffed, without stuffing or in the form of fillets or steaks. Place fish in greased shallow baking dish or pan. If desired, brush with melted margarine or butter and sprinkle with salt, pepper, herbs or lemon juice. Cook uncovered in 350°F oven until fish flakes easily with a fork. Whole fish also can be "planked" by cooking on a greased hardwood plank in the oven and served directly from the plank, garnished with a border of mashed potatoes or vegetables.

**Broil** fish fillets or steaks (about 1 inch thick) with tops 2 to 3 inches from heat. Dry surface of fish and brush with melted margarine or butter and season with salt and pepper if desired. Turn carefully halfway through cooking time and brush with melted margarine or butter. Broil until fish flakes easily with fork.

**Cook** fish or shellfish in liquid for soups or stews. Cover fish with water, broth or tomato juice; cover pan and heat to boiling. Reduce heat and simmer until done.

**Deep fry** fish in 2 to 3 inches of oil (375°F) in a deep-fat fryer or kettle or in 1½ to 2 inches of oil in a skillet. Coat fish for deep frying by dipping it into a mixture of flour, salt and pepper, then into beaten egg, followed by dry bread crumbs. Fry until golden brown.

**Panfry** fish by cooking in ⅛ inch of hot shortening over medium heat, turning once, until fish is lightly browned on both sides and flakes easily with a fork. Season fish steaks or fillets with salt and pepper, dip into beaten egg and then coat with flour before frying.

**Poach** fish fillets in a single layer in skillet with 1½ inches of water. Add sliced onion, sliced lemon, salt and pepper to water if desired. Fish fillets also can be poached in a combination of white wine and water with bay leaf added for flavor. Simmer uncovered until fish flakes easily with fork.

## Problems and Solutions

☐ *How can I eliminate the strong, slightly bitter taste from bluefish?*

Cut along each side of the dark, V-shaped strip of muscle in the center of the fish; remove. If left in fish to be frozen, the dark strip hastens rancidity.

☐ *How can I eliminate the muddy taste of freshly caught catfish?*

Catfish grown commercially would not have a muddy taste. Soak freshly caught catfish fillets three to four hours in vinegar water to remove some of the strong flavor.

☐ *How can I tell the difference between cod and scrod?*

Young cod, weighing less than 2½ pounds, are known as scrod. As a cod matures, it can grow to nearly eighty pounds in weight. In midwestern states, cod is sometimes known as the poor man's lobster. Other subspecies of the cod family are haddock, pollock and hake.

☐ *What is the difference between Atlantic blue soft-shell and hard-shell crabs?*

Atlantic blue soft-shell and hard-shell crabs are the same species, except the soft-shell crabs have been caught immediately after they shed their old hard shells. When their new shells harden, they are known as hard-shell blue crabs. The average crab sheds its shell three times a year as it grows.

## □ *How do I prepare a hard-shell crab?*

Live hard-shell crabs are available only in areas where they are caught, because they are extremely perishable. They are poached in salted or seasoned water. To cook a live crab, use tongs to grasp the live crab behind the back fins; plunge it headfirst into a kettle of boiling water. Simmer crabs uncovered for about twenty minutes. Remove cooked crab from the simmering water with tongs; place on a plate. The crab pictured below was purchased precooked.

**1. Pry** off the tail flap with your hands.

**2. Turn** crab right side up, pry up and tear off the top shell; discard.

**3. Pull** off the gray-white gills on either side of the crab; discard.

**4. Break** off the crab's claws and reserve.

**5. Twist** off legs, saving any meat attached.

**6. Break** the claw shells at the joints. With a nutcracker or small pliers crack the shell; pull out meat with nut pick or small fork.

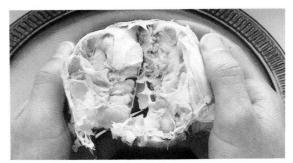

**7. Break** the crab's body into halves with hands or cut with a sharp knife; remove meat with nut pick or small fork. Break through the membrane with fingers and pick out meat from deeper pockets in each half of the body.

□ *What other fish recipes can be used for cooking croaker?*

Sea bass recipes can be used with croaker and croakers are delicious broiled or panfried. Found along the Atlantic coast, croakers are from the same family of fish as drums (both named for a noise they make at certain times) and can be substituted for the black drum fish in chowder.

□ *What is the difference between sea bass and freshwater bass?*

Sea bass is a large (up to ten pounds), firm, white fish found off the southern Atlantic and Mediterranean coasts and the east coast of the United States. Freshwater bass is a smaller (from one to five pounds), firm, lean fish found in northern lakes of the United States. Freshwater bass are classified as largemouth, smallmouth, rock, white or yellow bass.

□ *What is the difference between Dover sole and gray, lemon or rex sole?*

Dover sole, which comes from the English Channel and waters from Scandinavia to the Mediterranean, is imported to the United States. This is considered to be the original and authentic sole. Gray, lemon or rex sole are actually flounder.

□ *What other fish recipes can be used for cooking grouper?*

Recipes for sea bass or red snapper can be used with grouper which is a member of the sea bass family. Depending on locale, grouper may be marketed as jewfish, yellowfish, black grouper, speckled grouper or most commonly, as red grouper.

□ *What is the difference between haddock and halibut?*

Haddock is a small fish (two to five pounds) and a member of the cod family. When smoked, it is known as finnan haddie. Halibut is a large fish (fifty to one hundred pounds) and a member of the flounder family (flatfish). When poached, it has a delicate flavor.

□ *Why does some lake trout have a strong fishy taste?*

Because lake trout is a fat fish, it has a strong flavor if caught late in the year or in warm water. Lake trout is best eaten when freshly caught. If frozen, it should be used within a few weeks.

□ *How do I prepare and eat a whole lobster?*

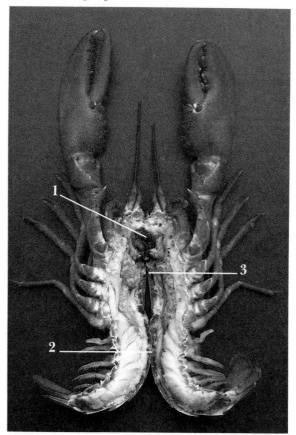

Whole, live lobsters are boiled in salted water. Use tongs to grasp the lobster behind the head, then plunge it headfirst into a large kettle of boiling water. Cover and heat to boiling; reduce heat. Simmer 10 minutes; drain. Place lobster on its back. Cut lengthwise into halves with sharp knife. Remove stomach (1), which is just behind the head, and intestinal vein (2), which runs from the stomach to the tip of the tail, Do not discard green liver or coral roe (3); they are regarded as delicacies and are eaten last. Crack claws with nutcracker or small pliers; pull out meat with small fork. Eat lobster meat with lemon juice or melted butter.

□ *How can I mask the fatty, strong taste of mackerel?*

Marinate mackerel in wine or lime juice and herbs before cooking; serve it in a tomato sauce with onions, garlic and herbs; or cook or smoke it over charcoal.

□ *What are some tips for buying or gathering mussels?*

The best months for harvesting mussels are late February, March, April and late August. The shells should be tightly closed; open shells indicate dead mussels.

□ *How do you open oysters in the shell?*

Scrub oysters in shells under running cold water. Break off thin end of shell with a hammer. Force blade of oyster (or table) knife or the pointed end of a bottle opener between halves of shell at broken end; twist knife and pull shells apart. Cut oyster at muscle to separate from shell. Open oysters over a bowl to save liquor in shell; strain liquor to remove bits of shell before using.

Oysters also can be opened in the microwave. After washing, arrange 6 oysters at a time with hinges toward outside on paper towel-lined plate. Cover tightly; microwave on high (100%) until shells open slightly, 1 to 1½ minutes. Remove oysters as they start to open. Hold oyster with hinge toward you; insert knife between shells near hinge, twist knife and open. Cut oysters at muscle to separate from shell.

□ *What are the varieties of Alaska salmon?*

There are five species of Alaska salmon. Chum salmon is lighter in color and less oily than other varieties; it weighs about nine pounds. King salmon (Chinook), usually sold in fillet form, is rich in oil; it weighs between eleven and thirty pounds. Pink salmon ranges in color from light to deep pink and contains very little oil; it weighs from two to five pounds. Silver salmon, usually sold in steak form, weighs from four to twelve pounds. Sockeye salmon is deep red in color and rich in oil; it weighs about six pounds.

□ *What are the varieties of scallops?*

There are two varieties of scallops. The sea scallop can grow a shell as large as eight inches in diameter with the eye, which is the edible portion, as large as two inches in diameter. The bay scallop can grow in a shell to a maximum of about four inches in diameter with the eye or edible portion about ½ inch across. Bay scallops are delicate in flavor and texture.

□ *In what ways can I serve pickled herring other than an appetizer?*

Add pickled herring, drained and chopped, to potato salad or to open-faced sandwiches with tomato and sour cream.

## ❑ *What is the difference between shad and shad roe?*

Shad is a member of the herring family, but larger and fatter than North Atlantic herring. It is caught in eastern rivers of the United States where they come to spawn, making their way up the Atlantic coast from Florida. Shad roe are the eggs of the female shad, which come in two separate pouches called a set which are connected by a thin membrane.

## ❑ *How do you clean cooked shrimp?*

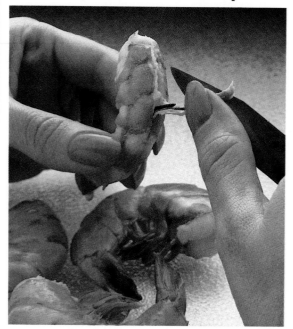

Peel the shells from the cooked shrimp. Using a small, pointed knife or a shrimp knife, make a cut the length of the outside curvature; remove black sand vein and wash shrimp.

## ❑ *How can I cook red snapper evenly when the fillets are of uneven thickness?*

Turn the thin ends under the fillets and bake the fish for even cooking. This method can be used with any fish fillets.

## ❑ *How is whitefish best prepared?*

Whitefish preparation is similar to that for lake trout, another fat fish. It can be baked or planked. See General Cooking Methods for Seafood and Fish, page 108.

## ❑ *How can I fillet a pike or other fish?*

Turn fish on its side; make a cut back of the gills straight down to the backbone. Turn knife blade flat; cut flesh along backbone almost to tail. (Except for tail portion, top fillet will be separated from the rest of the fish with the narrow rib cage still attached.)

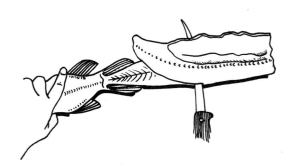

Without removing knife, lift the still-attached fillet away from backbone and entrails and flip it to the right so the flesh side is on top and the skin side on the bottom. Cut the fillet away from the skin in one piece by sliding the knife between the skin and the flesh. Use a sawing motion when cutting and press the knife blade close to the skin to remove as much flesh as possible.

Cut the rib cage from the fillet. Turn the fish over and repeat the above steps.

# Seasonings

Seasonings, whether basic salt and pepper or condiments, capers, herbs
or spices, give food special flavor and aroma. Herbs, seeds and spices
are discussed on page 65.

## Problems and Solutions

□ *Should salt be used to season meat before
or after cooking?*

Do not salt fresh meat before broiling, deep-
fat frying, panfrying or grilling over charcoal.
Salt draws juices from meat, preventing both
browning and sealing in of flavor. You can
season meat before roasting, but salt will not
penetrate more than ¼ to ½ inch. Salt meat
soups before cooking to extract meat juices,
which flavor the soups.

□ *How can I correct seasoning when I have
added too much salt to soup or gravy?*

Cook a quartered potato in liquid to absorb
the salt; remove the potato before serving.

□ *Can I make my own seasoned salt?*

Yes, you can. To ½ cup salt, add 1 tablespoon
each of celery salt, garlic salt and paprika and 1
teaspoon each of onion powder, dry mustard
and pepper. Mix ingredients in blender for 20
seconds; store in tightly covered container.

□ *What are capers?*

Capers are the unopened green flower buds
of a shrub grown near the Mediterranean.
They are pickled and used as a seasoning and
a condiment.

□ *What is the difference between black and
white pepper?*

Black pepper is ground peppercorns, which
are the dried berries of the pepper vine. Peppercorns also can be purchased whole, then
coarsely ground in a pepper grinder during
cooking or at the table. White pepper is
ground from ripened berries of the pepper
vine before they are dried, but after the husks
have been removed. White pepper has a
slightly less spicy flavor than black pepper. It is
used to season bland, light colored foods such
as eggs, cream soups and sauces, the appearance of which would be marred by the addition of specks of black pepper.

□ *What is the difference between red pepper
and paprika?*

Red pepper, also called cayenne pepper, is
ground from dried chili peppers and is very
pungent and hot. Paprika, ground from certain varieties of sweet red peppers, has a sweet
flavor but may be quite hot. The two peppers
sometimes are used together.

□ *What is MSG?*

Monosodium glutamate (MSG) is the sodium
salt of glutamic acid, fine white crystals, widely
used in food processing and in some recipes as
a flavor enhancer. MSG is commonly derived
from sugar beets or sugar cane through the
process of fermentation. This seasoning is
often used in Chinese cooking.

# Sweeteners

A sweet flavor can be given to food by other means than sugar. Corn syrup, honey, marshmallows and molasses are a few of the sweeteners most commonly used in cooking. In general, liquid sweeteners (corn syrup, honey and molasses) cannot be substituted for an equal amount of sugar in a recipe, because they add liquid as well as sweetening.

## Problems and Solutions

☐ *What is the difference between granulated sugar and superfine sugar?*

Granulated sugar is used at the table, for baking and in canning. Superfine sugar (more finely ground) is similar to English castor sugar and is used in beverages and for fine-textured cakes, meringues and frostings.

☐ *How can I make superfine sugar?*

Pour ½ cup granulated sugar into blender container. Cover and blend on medium speed 5 seconds; stir. Cover and blend an additional 5 seconds. Do not overblend or the sugar will be somewhat powdered.

☐ *How can I soften brown sugar that has turned hard?*

Place hardened sugar with half an apple or the heel of a loaf of fresh bread in an airtight container in the refrigerator for two or three days, or heat it uncovered for a few moments in a 250-300°F oven. Use immediately. Brown sugar also can be softened in the microwave by placing it in a microwaveproof bowl, covering tightly and microwaving on high (100%), checking every 30 seconds, until softened.

☐ *Can I substitute brown sugar for granulated sugar in a recipe?*

Brown sugar can be substituted for white sugar as a topping for fruits or hot cereals or for sweetening coffee, cream, sour cream or yogurt, but it is best to follow recipes exactly. In many recipes, brown sugar is given as an alternate ingredient for white sugar.

☐ *Can I substitute corn syrup for granulated sugar in a recipe?*

No, corn syrup is a liquid and cannot replace granulated sugar in a recipe without adjustment of other ingredients, especially in bakings. There is no substitution rule for corn syrup and granulated sugar in recipes.

☐ *Are light and dark corn syrups interchangeable in recipes?*

Yes, corn syrups can be used interchangeably. Light corn syrup is used when extra flavoring or darker color is not desired, as in candy and frosting recipes. Dark corn syrup is used for stronger flavor and darker color in bakings and as a table syrup.

☐ *Can I substitute honey for granulated sugar in a recipe?*

No, honey adds moisture to batter or dough and requires reduction of the amount of liquid in the recipe. There is no rule for substituting honey for granulated sugar.

☐ *How can I prevent marshmallows from becoming firm and stale?*

Store marshmallows in plastic bag in the freezer; cut them with scissors while frozen to add to salads and desserts.

# Vegetables

Crisp, plump, vitamin-rich vegetables, fresh in season, are an invitation to the imaginative cook to introduce exciting variety to mealtime. Many vegetables show off their brilliant colors, appealing shapes and distinctive flavors best when served raw as relishes or in huge, leafy salads. Others, particularly green vegetables, are most succulent when steamed or cooked only to the crisp-tender stage. And baked alone or in casseroles, vegetables make a handsome, substantial accompaniment to meat, fish and main dishes. Bring them into the kitchen fresh from the garden or the farmers' market, experiment with new combinations, collect and try unusual recipes. You'll never serve a dull dinner again. (See also Storing Foods, pages 152 and 154)

## Artichokes (Globe)

Choose a globe artichoke that is compact, heavy for its size with tightly clinging, fleshy leaves of a clear green color. A blistered, whitish color or a few brown-tipped leaves because of light frost do not affect quality.

Remove any discolored leaves and the small leaves at base of artichoke; trim stem even with base of artichoke. Cutting straight across, slice 1 inch off top; discard top. Snip off points of the remaining leaves with scissors. Rinse artichoke under cold water. Boil, steam or deep fry the "heart" according to recipe directions.

*Tip:* Season cooking water with lemon juice, clove of garlic and peppercorns if desired. Add a small amount of oil to make artichokes glossy.

*Tip:* Remove some of the center leaves and the choke before cooking if artichoke is to be filled with seafood or meat mixture and baked before serving.

*Tip:* To eat an artichoke, pluck leaves one at a time. Dip base of leaf into a sauce or lemon butter. Turn leaf meaty side down and draw between teeth, scraping off meaty portion.

When all outer leaves have been removed, a center cone of small, light-colored leaves covering the center choke will be exposed. Pull or cut off cone of leaves. Slice off fuzzy choke with knife and fork; discard. Cut the remaining "heart" into bite-size pieces.

## Artichokes (Jerusalem)

Jerusalem artichokes, also called sunchokes, are not true artichokes, but a tuber of a variety of sunflower plant. They have a gnarled appearance and a nutty taste similar to globe artichokes. Look for firm, hard, clean tubers.

Jerusalem artichokes should be scrubbed with vegetable brush in cold water; cut away knobs and small eyes with knife. Do not pare unless the skin is very tough. Jerusalem artichokes can be sliced and served raw in salads or with dips, or boiled, panfried or cooked and mashed and served hot.

*Tip:* Soak Jerusalem artichoke pieces in water with a small amount of lemon juice to prevent discoloration after cutting.

## Asparagus

Look for stalks that are straight, round, tender, crisp and green with compact, closed tips and only about an inch of woody base.

Break off tough end as far down as stalk snaps easily; wash asparagus. Remove scales if sandy or tough.

*Tip:* To cook asparagus spears, tie whole stalks in bundles with string and cook in 1 inch boiling salted water in deep, narrow pan or clean coffeepot until stalk ends are crisp-tender and tips are steamed tender.

# Bean Sprouts

Choose crisp, young sprouts with fresh (not dried out) tips and short stems.

Wash in cold water and eat raw or cooked in vegetable salads, main dishes and sandwiches.

# Beans (String, Stringless; see also Legumes (page 72)

Select long, crisp pods with fresh-looking tips and bright green or waxy yellow color. Beans may be flat, long and round or have a velvety pod, depending on variety.

Wash beans and remove ends. Leave beans whole (1) or cut French style (2) into lengthwise strips or crosswise (3) into one-inch pieces.

# Beans (Lima)

Lima beans should be broad, well-filled pods, dark green in color.

To shell lima beans, remove thin outer edge of pod with scissors. Beans will slip out.

# Beets

Look for firm, round, medium-sized beets with a deep red color. Beet tops should be fresh and green. (See also Greens, page 121.)

*Tip:* Cut off all but two inches of beet tops before cooking whole; avoid cutting the root too close, which causes beets to "bleed."

# Bok Choy (Chinese Chard)

Choose a long stalk with dark green leaves and firm, white ribs.

Cut off root end, separate stalks and remove wilted leaves.

*Tip:* Bok choy stalks can be sliced in thick pieces and cooked with leaves. Or the leaves may be cut from the ribs and cooked separately. Ribs can be sliced, used raw in salads, cooked in soups and stir-fried dishes.

# Broccoli

Choose firm, compact, dark green or purplish green clusters of small flower buds, with none sufficiently open to show yellow flowers. Stalks should be tender, firm and not too thick.

Trim off large leaves; remove tough ends of lower stems and wash broccoli. Trim into portion size before cooking.

*Tip:* If broccoli stems are more than one inch thick, make lengthwise gash for even cooking.

# Brussels Sprouts

Fresh sprouts are firm, compact and bright green and have no yellowing leaves, which indicate age.

Cut off stem ends, leaving enough stem to prevent outer leaves from falling off during cooking; wash sprouts before cooking.

# Cabbage (Green, Savoy and Red)

Look for well-trimmed heads that are firm and heavy for their size with fresh color. Early spring cabbage is not as firm as winter varieties, which are more suitable for storage. Red cabbage and green cabbage are alike except for their color.

Remove outside leaves; wash cabbage. Shred or cut into wedges.

*Tip:* Cook cabbage quickly in small amount of water. Exposure to air will cause loss of some nutrients; use soon after cooking.

*Tip:* When cutting cabbage into wedges, leave about ¼ inch of the core; it will hold the leaves together as they cook.

*Tip:* Add 2 tablespoons lemon juice or vinegar to cooking water to keep red cabbage from turning purple.

*Tip:* To separate leaves from cabbage head to use for stuffed cabbage rolls, remove core, cover cabbage with boiling water and let stand ten minutes. Remove leaves that have softened and repeat procedure. If leaves are not pliable enough to roll, continue to soak in boiling water about five minutes.

# Chinese Cabbage (Napa or Celery)

Choose long, firm heads with crinkly pale green leaves. Heads that are very large or firm may have a strong flavor.

Remove root ends, wash and use in salads, slaw and stir-fried dishes, or steam in small amount of water until crisp-tender.

# Carrots

Look for firm, nicely shaped orange carrots. Avoid carrots with large green area at top; this indicates sunburn.

Scrape carrots with vegetable parer or knife to save nutrients close to the skin.

*Tip:* Shredded carrots are delicious added to tossed salads or served cooked or uncooked as a vegetable.

*Tip:* Remove leafy green tops before storing carrots to preserve crispness.

# Cauliflower

Choose a white or slightly creamy white, firm and compact head; the size of the head has no relation to quality. If small green leaves are attached, they should be crisp and bright green in color, which indicate freshness.

Remove outer leaves and stalk at base; wash cauliflower. Break into small pieces and serve raw in salads. Leave whole or separate into flowerets before cooking.

*Tip:* Add a teaspoon of lemon juice to the cooking water to preserve white color.

# Celery (Golden Heart, Pascal)

Whether you buy Golden Heart, which is bleached white, or Pascal, which is green, choose crisp stalks with fresh green leaves. The inside of the stalks should be smooth; puffiness indicates poor celery.

Celery can be braised, whole or sliced, in beef broth until tender.

*Tip:* Celery leaves are nice for stuffings, soups, salads and garnishes.

# Celery Root (Celeriac)

Select firm, small roots; only the root is edible. Do not purchase celery root with sprouts, which indicate age.

Trim roots and top; pare. Serve raw in salads or marinate. Add to soups and stews or slice and panfry.

# Chayote (chah-YO-tee)

A member of the gourd family, chayote is a pear-shaped squash with one large seed. Choose dark green, smooth or ribbed hard chayote. The interior color is similar to that of honeydew melon.

Pare and substitute for summer or winter squash in recipes; add to salads, soups and main dishes. Panfry chayote or stuff and bake.

# Chinese Pea Pods (China Peas, Sugar Snap Peas)

Look for flat, crisp, smooth, bright green pods. Sugar peas are a little larger and heavier than China peas.

Wash pods; remove tips and strings from sugar peas. China peas can be eaten raw or stir-fried. Sugar peas can be steamed.

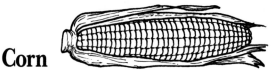

# Corn

Look for corn with fresh green husks and kernels that are tender, milky and plump. More than 200 varieties of sweet corn offer kernels that are white or yellow or a mixture of both on each cob.

*Tip:* Cook corn soon after picking or refrigerate it unhusked until ready to use. Remove husk and silk just before cooking.

*Tip:* For more tender corn, cook in unsalted water with 1 tablespoon sugar and 1 tablespoon lemon juice for each gallon of water.

# Cucumbers

Look for small, firm, fresh cucumbers with a deep green color; dull green or yellow color indicates poor quality. European cucumbers (about two inches in diameter and twelve to twenty inches in length) should be crisp and lighter green in color than common varieties.

Wash and slice cucumbers or cut lengthwise into sticks (do not pare) for relish trays or garnish for tall drinks. Pare and slice to use in sandwiches, or marinate and serve with sour cream. European cucumbers, which are almost seedless, can be used in the same way.

1. Chinese Cabbage
2. Spaghetti Squash
3. Celery Root
4. Jicama
5. Jerusalem Artichokes
6. Fennel
7. Daikon
8. Ginger
9. Bok Choy
10. Chayote

# Daikon (Japanese Radish)

Select clean, firm, white radish roots that are free from cuts and bruises.

Wash and grate for salads or slice for soup and vegetable trays.

# Eggplant

Eggplants are chiefly purple, but also yellowish white, red, white or striped, depending on variety. Choose smooth, firm, evenly colored eggplant, three to six inches in diameter.

Wash eggplant and slice just before cooking or cut into cubes or strips. Panfry, French fry, stuff or scallop eggplant.

*Tip:* Pare eggplant if to cook for only a short time; cook unpared for longer preparation.

# Fennel (Sweet Anise)

Fennel looks somewhat like celery but tastes and smells like licorice. Choose crisp, solid stalks with fresh, fernlike tops. The bulb should be well-developed without brown areas, which indicate age.

Slice fennel stalks and serve raw as an appetizer. Slice bulb, stalk and leaves and add to salads. Braise, boil or steam stalks, sliced into thin, lengthwise strips; serve hot with butter or in a sauce.

# Garlic (Fresh)

Select bulbs (sometimes called heads) of garlic with compact cloves and clean, dry skin.

Smack garlic clove with flat side of heavy knife to crack the skin, which then will slip off easily. Chop garlic with knife or crush in garlic press to use in cooking.

*Tip:* When cooked in soups and stews, whole garlic cloves become as mild in flavor as cooked onion.

*Tip:* Insert a wooden pick in whole clove of garlic that is to be removed from food after cooking; it will be easier to find and lift out.

*Tip:* Store unused peeled cloves or portions of cloves in a small jar of oil; cover and refrigerate for future use. Use the garlic-flavored oil in salad dressings.

# Gingerroot

Choose knobby gingerroot tubers that are firm, golden brown and fresh looking. The new sprouts on the side of the gingerroot have a more delicate flavor than the main root.

Grate, slice or shred pared gingerroot to use in fruit salads, fish or meat dishes and desserts.

*Tip:* Store gingerroot in a tightly covered container in the refrigerator or freezer.

*Tip:* Crush a small piece of unpeeled gingerroot in a garlic press to make ginger pulp and juice. Crush pared gingerroot between pieces of waxed paper with the flat side of a knife.

# Greens

Mild-flavored — Beet Top, Chicory (outer leaves), Collards, Dandelion greens, Spinach; Strong-flavored — Kale, Mustard, Swiss Chard, Turnip Top.

Wash greens several times in water, lifting out each time; drain.

*Tip:* Cook delicate greens a very short time in only the water that clings to the leaves.

# Jicamas (Hee-kah-mahs)

Jicamas resemble turnips and have a flavor like water chestnuts. Choose well-formed, small brown jicama roots; avoid large roots, which are woody.

Wash, pare and cut into strips, slices or cubes to serve raw with dips or in salads.

*Tip:* You can slice and boil, steam or panfry jicamas; prepare as you would potatoes.

*Tip:* Substitute sliced jicama for water chestnuts; they remain crisp when cooked.

# Kohlrabi (Cabbage Turnip)

Choose globular kohlrabi bulbs no larger than about three inches in diameter; avoid the tough and bitter large bulbs. Tops should be fresh and green in color.

Wash, trim stems, pare and cut in strips to eat raw or stir-fry.

*Tip:* Cook quartered bulbs, pared or unpared, in small amount of water until crisp-tender. Tops can be cooked like fresh greens.

# Lettuce

Choose iceberg lettuce heads that are firm but not hard, with no sign of rusty-looking tips. Other types of lettuce include butterhead with soft leaves and a delicate flavor, Romaine with long, dark green leaves and a stronger flavor than iceberg and leaf with a crisp texture and mild flavor.

*Tip:* To remove the core from iceberg lettuce, strike core end against a flat surface, twist and lift out.

# Mushrooms

Choose firm mushrooms with smooth, creamy white to light brown caps with closed "veil" around base of cap. Mushroom size is no indication of tenderness or quality.

Trim a thin slice from bottoms of stems that appear brown and dry. Rinse mushrooms carefully in cool water; blot with a towel. Do not rinse mushrooms until ready to use. Slice and serve raw in salads; stuff and broil or bake large, whole caps.

*Tip:* When serving mushrooms alone, cook quickly to retain shape, moisture and texture. Cook longer when mixed with other foods to impart full mushroom flavor.

*Tip:* Add 1 teaspoon lemon juice to 1 pound mushrooms when panfrying to retain white color and add flavor.

# Okra (Gumbo)

Choose tender, unblemished okra pods, green or white in color, long and thin or short and chunky, from two to four inches in length.

Wash and remove ends. Leave whole for baking, boiling or panfrying. Cut into ½-inch slices for soups and stews.

*Tip:* Cook okra rapidly to preserve flavor and prevent slippery consistency.

*Tip:* Avoid cooking okra in brass, copper or iron, which causes discoloration of pods.

# Onions (Dry, Green, Leeks or Shallots)

Choose dry onions (with yellow, white or red skins) that are firm, unblemished and well-shaped with dry, papery skins. Green onions, also known as scallions, should have crisp, green tops and two to three inches of white root. Leeks should have crisp, firm stalks with white bulbs and bright green tops; smaller leeks are more tender and are best served raw. Shallots have bulbs made up of cloves.

Slip the skins from dry onions under running cold water or pour boiling water over them before paring to prevent eyes from watering. Wash and trim green onions to remove roots and loose layers of skin. Leave about three inches of green top for flavor and color. Trim leeks by removing root, dry outer skin and blemished leaves. Wash leeks several times in water; drain. Slice and serve raw in salads or marinate for appetizers. Bake, broil or cook in liquid and use in stews, soups and sauces.

*Tip:* After eating onions, eat several sprigs of parsley that have been dipped in salt or vinegar to sweeten breath.

*Tip:* To keep onions whole and prevent inner section from slipping out while boiling, cut an "X" about ¼ inch deep in the stem end before cooking.

# Oyster Plant (Salsify)

A member of the sunflower family, oyster plant looks like a parsnip and has an oysterlike flavor. Choose medium-sized firm roots with heavy, grassy tops.

Trim, pare (before or after cooking) and cut in 2-inch pieces.

*Tip:* To prevent oyster plant from discoloring, drop pared and sliced pieces immediately into 1 tablespoon lemon juice to 1 pint of water before cooking.

# Parsley (See Herbs, Seeds and Spices, page 65)

## Parsnips

Look for firm, nicely shaped, slender small or medium-sized parsnips; wide parsnips may have a woody core.

Scrape or pare and leave whole or cut into halves or slices to panfry, deep-fat fry in batter coating or boil to mash, cream or add to soups.

## Peas, Green

Look for bright green, fairly large pea pods that are well-filled and tender.

*Tip:* For sweet, tender peas, wash, shell and cook quickly soon after picking.

## Peppers (Mild-flavored — Green and Red Bell; Hot-flavored — Chili and Cayenne)

Choose well-shaped, thick-walled and firm peppers with uniform color. Fresh bell peppers are mild and sweet fleshed. Hot peppers are often dried and sold in strings.

Wash peppers; remove stems and seeds by cutting into two sections from base almost to stem. Pull sections apart; stem end with most of the seeds will pop out. Cut sections into strips or dice. Remove stems, seeds and membranes to use whole; stuff and bake or slice into rings.

*Tip:* Remember, the larger the pepper, the milder its flavor; the smaller the pepper, the hotter to taste.

□ *How do I skin a pepper?*

**To remove** skin from pepper to be marinated or used in salads, hold pepper on a long-handled fork over a gas burner about one inch above a high flame. Turn pepper until it is evenly blistered and charred.

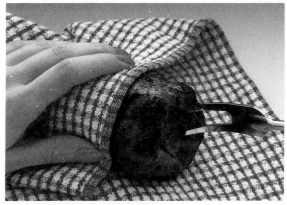

**Wrap** pepper in towel; let cool five minutes.

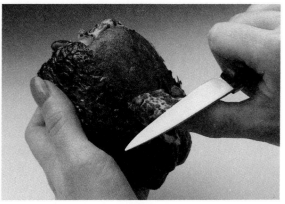

**Remove** skin with knife; remove stems, seeds and membrane. Three or four peppers can be roasted at one time in a broiler about one inch from heat, turning often.

# Potatoes (Round Red, Round White, Russet, Long White)

Look for fairly clean, smooth, firm and well-shaped potatoes to avoid waste in paring. Uniform size will ensure even cooking.

Wash potatoes or gently scrub with vegetable brush. Leave skins on whenever possible or pare thinly with a vegetable parer; remove eyes before cooking.

*Tip:* To retain white color of pared potatoes before cooking, toss them with ascorbic acid mixture or a small amount of lemon juice.

*Tip:* Avoid soaking potatoes in cold water for a long period, which causes vitamin loss.

*Tip:* Boiling potatoes in their skins, which can be eaten or slipped off easily after cooking, saves nutrients.

# Radishes (Red, White and Black)

Choose smooth, crisp, firm radish roots. Round radishes should be from one to four inches in diameter; long radishes range from three to six inches in length.

Wash all radishes under water. Trim excess stem and root of red radishes. Lightly scrape skin of white radishes; trim both ends. Serve as relishes, in salads and as a cooked vegetable.

*Tip:* Pare black radishes with vegetable parer before using.

*Tip:* Small radishes have sharper flavor; large radishes are easier to grate and chop.

*Tip:* Radishes can be cooked as a vegetable. Red radish slices retain color better when steamed rather than boiled.

# Rhubarb (See Fruits, page 61)

# Pumpkin

Choose pumpkins with bright orange color and firm rind; the smaller sizes usually have more tender flesh and less waste.

Halve or quarter pumpkin, remove seeds and stringy portions. Cut pumpkin into small pieces; cut off rind.

*Tip:* Cook pumpkins covered, in small amount of water until tender; drain, mash and let drain in strainer to remove excess liquid. Or cut into pieces and bake as you would hard-shelled squash.

*Tip:* One 5-pound pumpkin yields about 4½ cups of mashed, cooked pumpkin; just right for two 9-inch pies.

# Rutabagas

Choose heavy, well-shaped (round or elongated), smooth rutabagas. Size is not an indication of quality.

Wash, pare thinly and cut into ½-inch cubes or 2-inch pieces before cooking. Thin rutabaga slices can be served raw as a relish.

# Salsify (See Oyster Plant, page 122)

# Spinach (See Greens, page 121)

# Squash (Soft-shelled and Hard-shelled)

Choose soft-shelled squash (often called summer squash, although available all winter) that is firm and well-shaped with shiny, smooth skin. Choose hard-shelled squash (often called winter squash, although also available in late summer and fall) that is heavy with a hard, dark green or yellow-orange rind.

Wash soft-shelled squash and remove stem and blossom ends, but do not pare. Cut into ½-inch slices or cubes to boil, broil, panfry or bake. Cut hard-shelled squash in serving pieces with a chef knife; remove seeds and fibers with a serrated grapefruit spoon or tablespoon before baking or microwaving.

*Tip:* Spaghetti squash can be baked or microwaved whole if the shell is first pierced to allow steam to escape while cooking. To serve cooked spaghetti squash, cut squash into halves crosswise; scoop out seeds. Unwind spaghetti-like flesh with fork and serve as you would pasta.

*Tip:* Acorn and other small squash can be baked whole if the shell is first pierced to allow steam to escape while baking. Cut and remove seeds after baking.

# Sweet Potatoes (Jersey Sweets, Yams)

Look for smooth, even-colored skins and potatoes that are medium size, chunky and tapered toward the ends. Choose a light yellowish tan or fawn-colored skin for a dry sweet potato; a whitish tan to brownish red skin for a moist sweet potato.

Wash sweet potatoes; boil, bake or panfry.

*Tip:* Cooking sweet potatoes in their skins retains nutrients; skins slip off easily.

# Swiss Chard (See Greens, page 121)

# Tomatoes

Choose firm, well-shaped, fully ripe tomtoes that are heavy in relation to their size.

*Tip:* To peel, dip tomato into boiling water thirty seconds, then into cold water. Or scrape surface of tomato with dull side of knife to loosen; peel with sharp side of knife.

Speed up ripening of a slightly green tomato by placing in a brown paper bag; as the tomato ripens, it gives off a natural gas, ethylene, which hastens the ripening process when confined in a closed area.

# Turnips

Choose smooth, round, firm turnips with fresh tops.

Cut off turnip tops; wash and pare thinly, leave whole or cut into cubes.

*Tip:* Thin turnip slices can be served raw as a relish or in salads, as well as cooked.

*Tip:* Add 1 teaspoon sugar to cooking water to improve flavor and sweeten turnips.

# Water Chestnuts

Choose smooth, firm water chestnuts with dark brown skins.

Wash and pare; slice for salads, add to vegetables, casseroles and stir-fried main dishes.

*Tip:* Water chestnuts retain crisp texture after cooking.

# Kitchen
# Guidelines

# Cooking Basics

Good technique in cooking begins with understanding the terminology of recipes and knowing the correct way to prepare, combine and measure ingredients. And there's a helpful chart of yields and equivalents on page 132 for easy reference.

## Cooking Terms

Successful results from recipes depend on knowing the vocabulary. What do "to poach," "to fold" and "to lard" really mean?

### Preparing Ingredients

**Chop:** Cut into small pieces with knife. For example, chop nuts by holding end of knife tip on cutting board with one hand and moving blade up and down with other hand.

**Crush:** Press to extract juice or grind into fine particles. For example, crush a clove of garlic by hitting clove sharply with side of chef's knife (papery skin will slip off), then mash into paste with side of knife.

**Cube:** Cut into squares ½ inch or larger with knife. For example, cube a potato by cutting into strips and then cutting strips across to make cubes.

**Cut up:** Cut into pieces with scissors. For example, cut dried apricots by snipping into small pieces with scissors dipped into water to prevent fruit from sticking to blades.

**Dice:** Cut into squares smaller than ½ inch with knife. For example, dice carrots by cutting into strips and then cutting strips across to make small cubes.

**Grate:** Cut into tiny particles using small holes of grater. For example, grate lemon by rubbing fruit against small holes of grater.

**Mince:** Cut into very small pieces with knife. For example, mince garlic by chopping into very small pieces.

**Pare:** Cut off outer covering with knife or vegetable parer. For example, pare an apple by removing skin with knife.

**Peel:** Strip off outer covering. Peel an orange by holding it in one hand and removing peel from top to bottom with other hand.

**Score:** Cut surface of food about ¼ inch deep with knife to facilitate cooking, flavoring or tenderizing. For example, score fat surface of ham by cutting in uniform diamond pattern.

**Shred:** Cut into long, thin pieces using large holes of grater or a knife. For example, shred cheese by rubbing against holes of grater.

**Slice:** Cut into thin, flat pieces with knife. For example, slice a cucumber by cutting straight down, pushing knife slightly forward with each downstroke.

**Sliver:** Cut into long, thin pieces with knife. For example, sliver almonds by cutting into thin strips with small knife.

**Snip:** Cut into very small pieces with scissors. For example, snip parsley by cutting with scissors into measuring cup.

## Combining Ingredients

**Beat:** Mix ingredients vigorously with spoon, hand beater or electric mixer until smooth.

**Blend:** Mix ingredients until they are very smooth and uniform.

**Cut in:** Distribute solid fat in dry ingredients by cutting with pastry blender with a rolling motion or cutting with two knives until particles are desired size.

**Fold:** Combine ingredients lightly using two motions: first cut vertically through mixture with a rubber spatula; then slide spatula across bottom of bowl and up the side, turning mixture over. Continue down-across-up-over motion while rotating bowl ¼ turn with each series of strokes. For example, fold custard into stiffly beaten egg whites when making a dessert soufflé.

**Mix:** Combine ingredients in any way that distributes them evenly.

**Stir:** Mix ingredients with circular or figure-eight motion until of uniform consistency.

## Cooking

**Bake:** Cook in oven.

**Boil:** Heat until bubbles rise continuously and break on the surface. For rolling boil, the bubbles form rapidly.

**Braise:** Cook covered in small amount of liquid over low heat or in 300°F to 325°F oven.

**Brown:** Cook until surface of food changes color, usually in small amount of fat over medium heat.

**Cook and stir:** Cook rapidly in small amount of fat, stirring occasionally.

**Panfry:** Cook uncovered in small amount of fat.

**Poach:** Cook in hot liquid just below the boiling point.

**Roast:** Cook uncovered in oven on rack in shallow pan.

**Scald:** Heat liquid just below the boiling point. Tiny bubbles form at the edge.

**Simmer:** Cook in liquid just below the boiling point. Bubbles form slowly and collapse below the surface.

**Stir-fry:** A Chinese method of cooking uniform pieces of food in small amount of hot oil over high heat, stirring constantly.

## Special Terms

**Baste:** Spoon a liquid over food during cooking to keep it moist.

**Blanch:** Plunge food into boiling water for a brief time to preserve color, texture and nutritional value or to remove skin from fruit or nuts.

**Chill:** Refrigerate food to make cold.

**Cool:** Allow hot food or liquid to come to room temperature.

**Lard:** Insert strips of fat in uncooked lean meat to make it more tender and flavorful.

**Marinate:** Refrigerate food in a liquid that will tenderize it or add flavor.

**Reduce:** Boil liquid, such as gravy, uncovered to evaporate liquid until the desired consistency and to intensify flavor.

**Soften:** Let cold butter or margarine stand at room temperature until soft.

**Toast:** Brown food in oven or toaster.

# High Altitude Cooking

At 3500 feet or higher, air pressure is lower, liquid evaporates faster, water has a lower boiling point. Look for recipes with special high altitude directions; experiment with adapting your own favorites. Here are some guidelines to help you.

▸ Use specific high altitude recipes for baking.

▸ Follow specific package directions for mixes.

▸ As altitude increases, air pressure decreases. Water will boil more quickly but will never be as hot at boiling as it would at sea level, so count on longer cooking time for boiled foods.

**Cakes:** It may be necessary to reduce baking powder or baking soda and sometimes to use larger pans. Grease and flour pans well since cakes have a greater tendency to stick to pans at high altitude.

**Candy and Cooked Frosting:** Cook mixture at a temperature lower than the recipe states. Subtract 2°F for every 1000 feet above sea level.

**Deep-fried Foods:** To avoid food that is over-brown and undercooked, lower the cooking temperature about 3°F for every 1000 feet above sea level.

**Eggs:** Increase cooking time for eggs in the shell to compensate for altitude.

**Meats:** Meats cooked in liquid require longer cooking time. Meats cooked in the oven are not affected by high altitude.

**Vegetables:** Increase cooking time for fresh or frozen vegetables and dried beans, peas and lentils. Increase liquid, if necessary, to prevent scorching.

**Yeast Breads:** Rising time is shorter. Allow dough to rise *just* until doubled or use less yeast than recipe states.

Additional information can be obtained from libraries and other local resources.

# Measuring Ingredients

Rule one for successful cooking is to measure accurately, using proper equipment, which differs for dry and liquid ingredients.

**Butter or margarine:** For butter in block form, soften and pack firmly in nested measuring cup; level butter and remove excess with rubber spatula. For butter in stick form, cut desired amount (each stick equals ½ cup or 8 tablespoons).

**Buttermilk baking mix:** Spoon mix lightly into nested measuring cup; level top with metal spatula.

**Flour:** Dip nested measuring cup into bag or canister; level with metal spatula.

**Milk and other thin liquids:** Pour into glass measuring cup; check amount at eye level.

**Molasses and thick liquids:** Pour into glass measuring cup; check amount at eye level and remove contents with rubber spatula.

**Shortening:** Pack firmly in nested measuring cup; level and remove with rubber spatula.

**Shredded cheese, soft crumbs, raisins and nuts:** Pack lightly in nested measuring cup until full.

**Sugar:** For brown sugar, pack firmly in nested measuring cup; level with metal spatula. For granulated sugar, dip nested measuring cup into bag or canister; level with metal spatula. For powdered sugar, spoon lightly into nested measuring cup; level with metal spatula (press through sieve to remove lumps if necessary).

**Vanilla and other flavorings:** Pour into measuring spoon until full.

# Yields and Equivalents

| Food | If Your Recipe States | You Will Need Approximately |
| --- | --- | --- |
| Apples | 1 cup chopped | 1 medium |
| Bacon | ½ cup crumbled | 8 slices crisply fried |
| Bananas | 1 cup sliced | 2 small or 1 medium |
| Beans, green or wax | 3 cups 1-inch pieces | 1 pound |
| Beef | 1 cup ½-inch pieces | 5 ounces |
| Bread, white | 12 slices (⅝ inch thick) | 1 pound |
| | 1 cup soft crumbs | 1½ slices |
| Butter or margarine | 2 cups | 1 pound |
| Cabbage | 3½ to 4½ cups shredded | 1-pound head |
| Carrots | 1 cup ¼-inch slices | 2 medium |
| | 1 cup shredded | 1½ medium |
| | 1 cup ¼-inch diagonally sliced | 2½ medium |
| Cauliflower | 3 cups flowerets | 1 pound |
| Celery | 1 cup ¼-inch slices | 2 medium stalks |
| | 1 cup ¼-inch diagonally sliced | 2 medium stalks |
| | 1 cup thin sliced | 1¾ medium stalks |
| Cheese, American or Cheddar | 1 cup shredded | 4 ounces |
| cottage | 2 cups | 16 ounces |
| cream | 6 tablespoons | 3 ounces |
| | 1 cup (16 tablespoons) | 8 ounces |
| Chocolate, chips | 1 cup | 6 ounces |
| unsweetened | 8 squares (1 ounce each) | 8 ounces |
| Coconut | 1⅓ cups shredded | 4 ounces |
| | 1⅓ cups flaked | 4 ounces |
| Coffee, ground | 80 tablespoons | 1 pound |
| Corn | 1 cup kernels | 2 medium ears |
| Crab | ¾ to 1 cup flaked | 1 pound raw (in shells) |
| Cream, dairy sour | 1 cup | 8 ounces |
| whipping | 1 cup (2 cups whipped) | ½ pint |
| Crumbs, chocolate wafer | 1 cup finely crushed | 19 |
| graham cracker | 1¼ cups finely crushed | 16 squares |
| saltine cracker | 1 cup finely crushed | 28 |
| vanilla wafer | 1 cup finely crushed | 22 |
| Cucumber | 1 cup chopped | ¾ medium |
| Eggs, whites | 1 cup | 8 to 10 |
| whole | 1 cup | 4 to 6 |
| yolks | 1 cup | 12 to 14 |
| Escarole | 10 cups bite-size pieces | 1 medium head |
| Flour, all-purpose | 3½ cups | 1 pound |

## Yields and Equivalents

| Food | If Your Recipe States | You Will Need Approximately |
|------|----------------------|----------------------------|
| Green pepper | 1 cup chopped | 1 medium |
| Lemon, juice | 2 to 3 tablespoons | 1 medium lemon |
|   peel | 1½ to 3 teaspoons grated | 1 medium lemon |
| Lettuce | 6 cups bite-size pieces | 1-pound head |
| Macaroni | 4 cups cooked | 2 cups uncooked (6 to 7 ounces) |
| Marshmallows | 10 miniature | 1 large |
| | 1 cup | 11 large or 110 miniature |
| Mushrooms | 3 cups ¼-inch slices | 8 ounces |
| Noodles, egg | 4 to 5 cups cooked | 4 to 5 cups uncooked (8 ounces) |
| Nuts (without shells), | | |
|   almonds | 3½ cups | 1 pound |
|   peanuts | 3 cups | 1 pound |
|   pecans | 4 cups | 1 pound |
|   walnuts | 4 cups | 1 pound |
| Oats, quick-cooking | 1¾ cups cooked | 1 cup uncooked |
| Olives, pimiento-stuffed | 1 cup sliced | 15 large or 36 small |
|   ripe | 1 cup sliced | 48 medium |
| Onions, green | 1 cup sliced | 9 (with tops) |
|   white | ½ cup chopped | 1 medium |
| Orange, juice | ⅓ to ½ cup | 1 medium orange |
|   peel | 1 to 2 tablespoons grated | 1 medium orange |
| Potatoes | 1 cup ½-inch pieces | 1 medium |
| | 1 cup ¼-inch pieces | 1 medium |
| | 1 cup grated | 1 medium |
| Radishes | 1 cup sliced | 12 |
| Rice, converted | | |
|   (parboiled) | 3 to 4 cups cooked | 1 cup uncooked |
|   precooked (instant) | 3 cups cooked | 1½ cups uncooked |
|   regular (white) | 3 cups cooked | 1 cup uncooked |
|   wild | 3 cups cooked | 1 cup uncooked |
| Shortening | 2 cups | 1 pound |
| Shrimp | 2 cups (¾ pound) cooked | 1½ pounds raw (in shells) |
| Spaghetti | 4 cups cooked | 7 to 8 ounces uncooked |
| Strawberries | 4 cups sliced | 1 quart |
| Sugar, brown | 2¼ cups (firmly packed) | 1 pound |
|   granulated | 2 cups | 1 pound |
|   powdered | 4 cups | 1 pound |
| Tomatoes | 1 cup chopped | 1 medium tomato |
| Zucchini | 2 cups sliced | 1 medium |

# Equipment

Save energy and promote safety first in your kitchen. Match pans to burner size. Only preheat the oven when necessary. Here's how to rescue frozen food when the power fails, and how to care for and sharpen knives. There's a right way to use most appliances. Be sure you know the rules.

## Appliances
### Ranges

#### Range-Top Energy Savers

▶ Use the smallest possible pan for the quantity of food to be cooked in order to reduce area heated. Use large pans on large cooking units and small pans on small units.

▶ Use minimum amount of liquid to reduce cooking time. Use low heat and pans with tightly fitted covers to reduce cooking time.

#### Range-Top Safety

▶ Turn pan handles so that they do not extend over edge of range, where they can be easily tipped off, or over another heating unit, where they can become too hot to handle.

▶ Make sure all burners and units are turned off when pans are removed.

▶ Give constant attention to the heating of oil for deep frying on range top.

### Oven Energy Savers

▶ Preheat oven only when specified in recipe. Roasts, casseroles, most vegetables and foods requiring more than an hour of cooking time can be started in a cold oven.

▶ Always preheat oven for cakes, pastries, breads, quick breads and soufflés. Most ovens will preheat within 10 minutes.

▶ Check the accuracy of your oven's temperature occasionally; a variance of even 20°F can affect the quality of your baking. If you have reason to believe that your oven thermostat is not registering correctly, place a portable oven thermometer on rack centered in oven. Set oven temperature, wait 10 to 15 minutes and then check thermometer. If temperatures do not agree, adjust oven setting to match the thermometer reading. Maintain the adjustment until necessary repairs have been made.

▶ Use your oven to capacity. Plan a complete oven meal or bake several foods at one time. Avoid overloading the oven since air must circulate freely.

▶ When baking on 1 rack, arrange the oven rack so top of food is about the same distance from top of the oven as the rack is from the bottom. Allow extra space at top for foods that rise above pan.

▸ Cook or bake 2 or more foods at one time. A 1½- to 2-inch clearance all around each baking pan will permit air to circulate and foods to bake evenly.

▸ Close oven door promptly after inserting food to prevent loss of heat; do not open during baking time. Set an oven timer for the minimum baking time stated in the recipe. If necessary, reset timer and bake food until maximum time stated in recipe.

### Oven Safety

▸ Wear oven mitts or use pot holders and pull the oven rack part way out when checking food for doneness.

### Broiler Energy Savers

▸ Do not preheat the broiler. Set oven control to broil and/or 550°F; place food on rack in broiler pan.

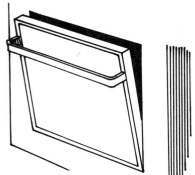

▸ Correct distance from the heat unit or gas flame and timing are important for successful broiling. The door must be left ajar on some electric ranges or thermostat will cause broiler to switch off when a certain temperature is reached. In gas ranges, broiling is done with door closed.

## Refrigerators

Your refrigerator, which should be set at 40°F, offers convenient short-term storage but is less effective than your freezer in stopping all bacterial activity. To take full advantage of your refrigerator:

▸ Buy fresh food of top quality.

▸ Be sure to refrigerate fresh food immediately after purchase.

▸ Store refrigerated food within the recommended storage period.

### Defrosting and Cleaning

▸ If the refrigerator is not self-defrosting, defrost when frost is ¼ inch thick for efficient use of energy. Wipe the interior with a damp sponge dipped in a solution of 3 tablespoons baking soda to 1 quart of warm water.

▸ Wipe refrigerator door gasket with soapy water, rinse and dry. If the door seals well, less energy will be used to operate.

▸ Vacuum the condenser fins at back of refrigerator periodically; accumulated dust will shut off circulation and increase energy used to operate refrigerator.

▸ Leave refrigerator door open if the appliance is not operating.

# Freezers

▸ When you want to freeze food in large quantities, guard against a rise of temperature in your freezer. Reduce freezer temperature to -10°F or lower about 24 hours before you add a large amount of unfrozen food; it will be frozen solid in 10 to 12 hours.

▸ Wrap all food in freezer wrap, label and date before freezing. Keep an inventory of the contents of the freezer, and use the longest-stored foods first.

▸ Store small packages of food together in one plastic bag so that they will be easy to locate.

▸ At any one time, freeze only as much food as you can place against a freezing surface. Arrange food packages at least 1 inch apart to allow air to circulate. Once frozen solid, the packages can be stacked.

## Power Failure

In case of power failure or mechanical defect, keep the freezer closed. In a full freezer that is kept at 0°F, little or no thawing will take place within the first 12 to 20 hours. A half-full freezer will keep food cold for about 24 hours. Twenty-five pounds of dry ice added to a 10-cubic-foot freezer will keep foods frozen up to 3 full days.

When power is restored, check foods to determine extent of loss. Dispose of any food that is off-color or has an off odor. Meats that retain ice crystals can be refrozen safely but with some loss of quality. Never taste suspect meat, poultry or other foods.

# Microwave Ovens

Microwaves are simply a form of radiant energy, much like radio and television waves. A magnetron tube converts household electricity into microwaves for cooking. They bounce off the metal walls of the microwave, pass through nonmetal materials such as glass, paper, plastics and wood, and are absorbed by food containing fat or moisture. The microwave, properly used, is one of the safest appliances in the home. The government has established strict limits on the level of energy emitted by the oven. When the set time has elapsed or when the door of the microwave is opened, the magnetron turns off and microwaves are no longer produced.

## Microwave Energy Savers

▸ Microwave cooking is a great energy saver because of its speed.

▸ No preheating is necessary in a microwave.

▸ Cook or reheat in the same dish from which you eat to save dishwasher energy.

## Microwave Safety

▸ While the microwave is a safe appliance, it is best to follow the manufacturer's safety instructions in the use and care guide that comes with your particular model.

▸ Clean the door seal with a soapy sponge, rinse and dry completely. A clean door that closes properly is important for safe use of your microwave.

## Convection Ovens

In the convection oven, hot air kept at a uniform temperature constantly recirculates, bombarding the food. Cooking is done at a lower temperature more quickly than in a conventional oven but not as quickly as in a microwave. Convections are powered by electricity or gas and can be placed on a counter or built into a wall.

▶ Do not let the appliance cord or plug get wet; disconnect it from outlet when cleaning convection oven.

## Toaster Ovens

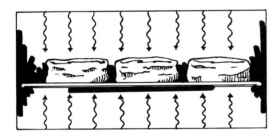

The counter top toaster oven is a convenience appliance that toasts bread on both sides at once, browns English muffins, heats sandwiches and bakes small items. There are many models available to fit varying needs.

## Food Processors

A food processor is a compact counter top machine that performs many time-consuming chores and simplifies complicated kitchen procedures. It chops, slices, shreds and mixes food, chops and slices meat, kneads dough and purées pâtés.

Food is placed directly in the bowl or dropped through the feed tube. A pusher directs the food toward the blade, which determines the final size and shape. The order in which foods are added and the on-and-off procedure prevent food from being overprocessed.

If you overprocess food, remember that you can use fruit as a sauce or beverage, nuts or shrimp in spreads or dips and vegetables as a base for soup.

## Pressure Cookers

A pressure cooker is a saucepan with a lid that seals into place for cooking foods under pressure. Foods can be pressure-cooked in about one-third the time of conventional methods. Less tender cuts of meat can be tenderized in a shorter time while saving fuel and retaining vitamins and minerals.

Follow manufacturer's directions for your particular model pressure cooker.

Food that is pressure-cooked will be done in about one-third the time of the same food that is conventionally cooked.

When control jiggles, the desired amount of pressure has been reached. Reduce heat so the control jiggles only occasionally. Count cooking time from the time the control first starts to jiggle.

Have the seal and pressure gauge on a pressure canner professionally checked regularly for accuracy.

Remove cooker from heat at end of cooking time and cool pan to reduce pressure. Handles slide apart easily when pressure is completely reduced.

# Bakeware

Furnishing a new kitchen? Forget about gadgets and frills for now. Concentrate on these essentials for day-to-day baking and cooking. Buy good quality ware in the recommended materials. It will serve you well for many years.

## Basic Bakeware

1. Cookie sheets
2. Baking pans (8-inch square and 13 × 9 × 2 inches)
3. Covered casseroles (1-, 2- and 3-quart)
4. Loaf pan (9 × 5 × 3 inches)
5. Baking pan (9-inch square)
6. Round layer pans (8 or 9 × 1½ inches)
7. Tube pan (10 × 4 inches)
8. Custard cups
9. Pie plate (9 × 1¼ inches)
10. Jelly roll pan (15½ × 10½ × 1 inch)
11. Roasting pan (with rack)
12. Muffin pan

**Aluminum baking pans** are excellent conductors of heat and produce uniform browning of food. When purchasing layer cake pans and cookie sheets, choose shiny pans, which reflect heat to produce light, delicate crusts. Keep shiny aluminum pans bright by cleaning with a soap-filled pad. For breads or pies, choose dull or anodized pans to produce crisp, brown crusts.

**Nonstick finishes** make cleanup easy. For ease in removing cake, greasing the pans is recommended for all cakes except angel food or chiffon, which must cling to the pan to rise. Wash nonstick finishes in hot, soapy water and never scour the surface; scratching destroys the finish and makes it less effective.

**Glass baking dishes** absorb and hold heat well, are easy to clean and can be used for storage of all kinds of food. Glass is preferred for a crisp, brown crust.

# Cookware

## Basic Cookware

Covered skillets (8-inch and either 10- or 12-inch)

Covered saucepans (1- and 2-quart and either 3- or 4-quart)

Dutch oven

## Kinds of Materials

**Cast aluminum** is heavy-gauge, durable and retains heat well.

**Stamped aluminum** is lighter weight than other materials, less expensive and conducts heat well.

**Porcelain enamel** on heavy-gauge aluminum offers an easy-to-clean finish; porcelain enamel on steel gives an odor- and stain-resistant surface but can chip or craze when exposed to sudden high heat; procelain enamel on cast iron is heaviest, most durable, highest priced and can be used on range top, in the oven and at the table.

**Stainless steel** is durable, easy to clean and resists staining, pitting and corrosion; aluminum-clad gives rapid, even heating; copper-clad is excellent for low-heat cooking, although bottoms require some care to keep them shiny.

**Cast iron** heats easily and retains heat for a long time, but it must be seasoned.

**Nonstick finishes** come in two varieties. The less expensive kind is applied to the surface and will eventually wear away. The more expensive kind is fired on and longer lasting. Follow manufacturer's directions for initial seasoning and general care.

# Utensils

## Basic Knives

**1. Paring knife** for paring, trimming and cutting. These knives come in a variety of shapes with both rounded and pointed tips. Blades usually are 2½ to 3 inches long. Can be used for paring fruits, trimming blemishes, cutting radish roses, deveining shrimp.

**2. Utility knife** for cutting, slicing and coring. These knives come in an assortment of shapes with straight or serrated edges. Can be used for cutting pies and sandwiches, slicing cookie dough, coring pears, sectioning oranges.

**3. Boning knife** for boning, cutting and slicing. These knives are used for close cutting, using the tip of the knife. Blades are usually slim and pointed and the handles are broad. Can be used for boning chicken and fish, cutting pineapples and spareribs, slicing tomatoes, onions and potatoes.

**4. Steel** for sharpening knives.

**5. French chef's knife** for chopping, cutting and slicing. These knives have heavy triangular blades and come in various lengths. Can be used for chopping celery and nuts, slicing watermelon, cutting large, hard vegetables (squash).

**6. Carving knife** for slicing, carving and cutting. These knives have long, curved blades. Can be used for slicing meats and large, soft vegetables (eggplant), carving turkey, cutting pastry dough.

**7. Slicing knife** for slicing, cutting and shredding. These knives have serrated or toothed edges. Can be used for slicing bread, cutting cakes, shredding cabbage.

## Care of Your Knives

*Tip:* Store knives in a rack, sheath, box or knife block, inaccessible to children.

*Tip:* Use a wooden cutting board to protect the edge of the knife except when cutting raw meat, poultry or fish, which should be cut on a nonabsorbent plastic board for food safety and cleanliness.

*Tip:* Never expose blades to high heat or open flame or use them to lift bottle caps or jar lids, to cut paper or to open packages.

*Tip:* Sharpen knives frequently with a good steel, stone or electric knife sharpener.

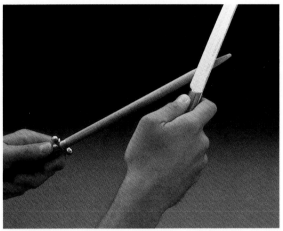

Hold the sharpening steel in one hand, horizontally at a 45° angle from your body. Grasp the knife handle in your other hand, resting the edge of the blade heel at a 20° angle near the point on the top of the steel.

With light pressure, draw the blade toward you (along the top of the steel). Repeat with the other side of the knife blade on the underside of the steel. Repeat alternately 3 or 4 times on each side. With practice, you will develop a rhythmic motion which results in smooth, even sharpening.

*Tip:* Keep stainless steel knives shiny by rubbing with a piece of lemon peel or a soft cloth moistened with rubbing alcohol.

## Basic Measuring Tools

Nested dry measuring cups (¼-, ⅓-, ½- and 1-cup)

Liquid measuring cup (1-cup)

Measuring spoons (¼-, ½- and 1-teaspoon and 1-tablespoon)

Metal spatula (for leveling off ingredients)

## Basic Utensils

Mixing bowls of assorted sizes for beating eggs, mixing cakes and refrigerating food

Cutting boards (wooden for breads and cooked meats and nonabsorbent plastic for raw meat, fish and poultry)

Wooden spoons, plastic or metal mixing spoon, slotted spoon

Plastic utensils for nonstick pans

Long-handled fork

Rubber spatulas (wide and thin)

Rolling pin and stockinet cover, pastry cloth plus pastry blender

Colander for draining spaghetti

Strainer for sifting powdered sugar over cakes and cookies

Grater/shredder

Egg beater or hand electric beater

Kitchen scissors and/or poultry shears for cutting up chicken and removing thorny tips from artichoke leaves

Tongs for turning meat during cooking or serving corn-on-the-cob

Vegetable brush

Openers (can, bottle and jar)

Pastry brush and basting brushes (small paintbrushes) for basting poultry and greasing pans and casseroles

Pot holders or oven mitts

## Special Utensils

Collect these utensils as your cooking expertise grows. Many do double duty for other kitchen tasks.

1. Funnel for pouring liquids into containers with small tops

2. Pepper mill for grating fresh pepper

3. Gelatin molds and ring molds

4. Pancake turner

5. Mallet or meat tenderizer for making meat cutlets and crushing garlic

6. Egg slicer

7. Heavy thread or dental floss for cutting raised yeast dough into cinnamon rolls or cutting slices of crumbly blue cheese

8. Thermometers for roasted meats, candy and deep-frying

9. Cutters for biscuits and cookies or can be used for forming hamburgers or shaping round fried eggs

10. Kitchen timer

11. Wire whip for delicate sauces and custard

12. Garlic press for crushing garlic, ginger-root and onion

13. Chopsticks for turning food in deep-fat

14. Wooden picks for testing cakes

15. Ladle for soups and gravies

16. Cheese cutter

17. Baster to skim fat from soups and stews

18. Ruler for measuring yeast dough before forming loaves and for pastry circles

19. Ice-cream scoops in several sizes for desserts, cookies, and scooping muffin batter into cups

20. Metal skewers for kabobs and to contain stuffing in turkey

21. Pastry bag and tubes for decorating

22. Apple corer for coring apples and pears

23. Vegetable parer for paring vegetables and making chocolate curls

# Shopping Secrets

Shopping for top value in quality, nutrition and cost is a science today. Look for additional information under individual food listings in Tips and Techniques.

## Shopping Guides

*Tip:* Plan menus by the week so that one shopping trip will provide essentials with an occasional quick stop for perishables.

*Tip:* Keep a running shopping list and add items as your supply of staples runs low.

*Tip:* Organize your shopping list by categories to match the traffic pattern of your favorite store; you will save time and steps.

*Tip:* Use a purse-size calculator to figure best buys by weight or for a running total of selections to keep your spending within limits.

### Breads

Have you ever wondered how many slices in a loaf of bread? Use this guide when you plan sandwiches for parties or lunch boxes to figure the average number of slices in a loaf.

| Bread Slices per Loaf | |
|---|---|
| Loaf Weight | Slices |
| White | |
| 1¼ pounds | 19 |
| 1½ pounds | 24 |
| 2 pounds | 28 |
| 2 pounds, (thin sliced) | 36 |
| Whole wheat | |
| 1 pound | 16 |
| 2 pounds, (thin sliced) | 28 |
| Rye | |
| 1 pound | 23 |

### Canned Foods

Most canned foods are packed and priced according to their quality. A U.S. Department of Agriculture (USDA) grade shield may appear on the label.

Buy cans that are in good condition. Avoid cans that are dented, rusted or bulging at the ends; they may not be safe.

Buy the size of canned goods that fits your needs; find the most economical buy by comparing weights or contents and unit costs.

Compare different brands of canned foods as well as generic brands. Unless appearance is important such as "whole" versus "pieces," there is no difference in safety or food value; only the flavor sometimes varies.

### Dairy Foods

Have you ever opened a food package and found that the contents were not fresh? It need not happen now that many dairy products are dated as a guide to freshness.

#### Cheese

The labels on natural cheese and pasteurized process cheese carry a variety of information:

**Process** cheese is cheaper and melts more readily than natural cheese. Cheese purchased by the block is less expensive than individually wrapped slices, although process cheese and wrapped slices keep longer than the block cheese.

#### Cream

The U.S. Food and Drug Administration (USFDA) standards specify minimum milkfat requirements for each type of cream.

Half-and-half contains between 10 and 18 percent milkfat.

Heavy whipping cream must contain at least 36 percent milkfat.

## Milk

Grade A milk and milk products are pasteurized. Whole milk is usually homogenized and fortified with vitamins.

Skim and lowfat milks have a lower level of milkfat than whole milk and usually offer a better value than whole milk.

## Eggs

What's your Egg I.Q.? Brown eggs versus white — which have more food value? Actually, there is no difference; shell color is determined by the breed of hen that lays the egg. While Bostonians buy brown eggs and New Yorkers prefer white, taste and nutrients are identical in both.

Look for eggs in shells that are clean and whole. If a shell cracks between the market and home, use it as soon as possible in a fully cooked dish.

Although freshness does not affect the nutritive content of an egg, it does influence the cooking quality. Commercially produced eggs reach supermarkets within hours of leaving the laying house. If the market and consumer handle and refrigerate them properly, they will still be fresh when used.

There is very little difference in quality between Grades AA and A, and there is no difference in nutritive content. Almost no Grade Bs are sold in the retail market.

Egg sizes are based on the weight per dozen: Jumbo (30 ounces), Extra Large (24 ounces), Medium (21 ounces) and Small (18 ounces). The price of eggs is determined by quality, size and time of year.

## Fats and Oils

Look on packages of butter for the USDA grade shield, which means the butter has been tested and graded by experienced government graders.

If you substitute margarine for butter in recipes, buy solid, not whipped, margarine.

Buy cooking and salad oils in small quantities to avoid flavor changes during long storage.

## Fruits

Buy firm, fresh fruits that appear clean and free from defects, bruises and blemishes.

Buy fruits by size and variety for the purpose intended and buy only what you need and will use without waste.

Select fruit for best eating quality rather than outer appearance; appearance does not always denote fine quality.

Many fruits are in season year-round but cost less during months when most plentiful.

| Seasonal Buying Guide | |
|---|---|
| Fruit | Peak Season |
| Apples | September to April |
| Apricots | June and July |
| Avocados | All year |
| Bananas | All year |
| Blueberries | June to August |
| Cantaloupe | May to October |
| Cherries, sweet | June to August |
| Cranberries | September to February |
| Grapefruit | October to June |
| Grapes | June to January |
| Kiwi fruit | June to March |
| Lemons and limes | All year |
| Melons, honeydew | March to November |
| Nectarines | June to October |
| Oranges | November to July |
| Peaches | June to October |
| Pears, Bartlett | July to December |
| D'Anjou | October to June |
| Pineapple | April to June |
| Plums | June to October |
| Pomegranates | September to January |
| Raspberries | June to August |
| Rhubarb | January to August |
| Strawberries | May to July |
| Tangerines | November to March |
| Watermelon | May to September |

## Legumes (Dried Beans, Peas, Lentils)

Buy dried beans, pictured (1) above, peas (2), or lentils (3), in see-through packages so you can consider these factors:

▸ A bright, uniform color indicates freshness.

▸ Uniform size results in even cooking.

▸ Unbroken seed coats and absence of foreign material in the bag are signs of a high-quality product that has no insect damage.

▸ Read the label for the common name of the product, the weight and instructions on preparation and serving.

## Meats

Is the meat you buy safe to eat? To be certain that it comes from healthy animals and has been processed under sanitary conditions, choose only government-graded meats that are stamped, "Inspected by USDA."

Buy meats from a refrigerated case; the thermometer in the case should read 40°F.

Buy meat according to this guide (increase amounts for hearty appetites):

**Boneless** meat — about ¼ pound per serving

**Bone-in** meat — about ½ pound per serving

**Large bone-in** or very bony meat — ¾ to 1 pound per serving

Plan on leftovers from large cuts of meat that require long cooking.

Some meats are more plentiful during certain seasons: lamb in the spring, and beef and pork in the winter. They are usually less expensive then; watch for advertised seasonal specials.

Less costly cuts of meat have the same nutritional value as more expensive cuts. Braising, stewing, marinating, using commercial tenderizers or cooking in the pressure cooker will tenderize many economical cuts.

Watch your meat case for unadvertised or midweek specials.

Buying a quarter or side of beef can be either a money-saving or a money-losing proposition, depending on retail yields and purchase cost.

Lamb and pork are generally processed from young animals and, therefore, vary less in quality than beef.

## Poultry

Look for the USDA grade shield on the poultry label or on a tag attached to the wing. The shield certifies that the poultry has been graded for wholesomeness and quality.

Young birds are more tender than older ones and may be labeled "young."

Most kinds of ready-to-cook poultry are available as parts or in whole, halved and quartered forms. Some kinds are also available as boneless roasts and rolls. There is a size and form to suit every purpose.

Learn the hows and whys of poultry-buying. For instance, what is the best bargain in chickens? The best bargain is the whole chicken; cut-up chicken costs more per pound. Also, the bigger the bird, the more meat it offers in proportion to bone.

Since whole chickens usually cost less than chicken parts, buy several when they are on special and cut them up yourself (see page 100). You can then freeze packages of chicken parts in the right quantities for your needs.

Plan about ½ pound chicken per serving, ¾ pound turkey per serving (from turkeys under 12 pounds) and ½ pound turkey per serving (from turkeys 12 pounds and over).

# Seafood (Fish and Shellfish)

Unless you live in a seaport and go down to the boats for the catch of the day, "fresh" fish in markets has been briefly frozen for shipping. These are best buys when in plentiful supply.

## Availability of Fresh Saltwater Fish by Months

| Month | Heavy Supply | Plentiful | Generally Available |
|-------|--------------|-----------|---------------------|
| **January** | Tilefish, mullet, sea bass, pollack, Spanish mackerel | | Sea trout, bluefish |
| **February** | Flounder | Watch promotions on canned and frozen fish | King and Spanish mackerel, red snapper, croaker |
| **March** | Flounder, tilefish, cod | Frozen ocean perch may be on special | Scrod, grey sole, king and Spanish mackerel, porgy, striped bass |
| **April** | Shad, halibut, striped bass | Cod, scrod, flounder, grey sole, tilefish, red snapper, wolffish, grouper, whiting, smelt | |
| **May** | Lobster, scallops, mussels (peak supplies from May to October) | | Lemon and grey sole, flounder, ocean perch, sea bass, red snapper, tilefish, wolffish, halibut |
| **June** | Grey sole, halibut, sea bass | Frozen ocean perch, salmon, flounder and sole may be on special | Cod, perch, porgy, bluefish, flounder, fluke, Atlantic and king salmon, red snapper, fresh tuna |
| **July** | | Cod, flounder, bluefish, whiting, perch, halibut, red salmon, sea scallops | Swordfish, fresh tuna, shellfish |
| **August** | Bluefish, cod | Flounder, mackerel, sea scallops, butterfish, halibut, red snapper | |
| **September** | | | Flounder, hake, silver salmon, spot, swordfish, bluefish, sea trout, mussels, scallops, lobsters, clams |
| **October** | Oysters from Chesapeake Bay | Hake, cod, flounder, lemon sole, mullet, red snapper, bluefish, porgy, mackerel, silver salmon | |
| **November** | Hake, flounder, sea trout, porgy | | Mullet, pollack, striped bass |
| **December** | Pollack, mullet | Cod, croaker, whiting | Eel, red hake, red snapper, Spanish mackerel |

When buying whole fresh fish, look for bright, clear, bulging eyes, firm flesh that is elastic when touched and a fresh odor.

Buy frozen fish that is frozen solid with no discoloration and little or no odor. It should be well wrapped when frozen.

Wide variations in price and availability are the rule in fresh fish markets.

Did you realize how high fresh fish is in protein content? Only 2 to 3 ounces without bones or shells provide the protein needed for 1 serving. Here are suggested amounts of fish to buy per serving.

### How Much Fish to Buy

| Form of Fish | Amount Per Serving |
|---|---|
| Whole fish (not dressed) | 1 pound |
| Drawn fish (whole but cleaned and gutted) | ¾ pound |
| Dressed fish (or pan-dressed and weighing less than 1 pound) | ½ pound |
| Fish steaks (cut in ¾-inch slices from large dressed fish) | ⅓ pound |
| Fish fillets (nearly boneless — sides cut lengthwise from backbone) | ¼ pound |
| Fish butterfly fillets (double fillets connected by skin) | ¼ pound |
| Fish sticks (from frozen blocks of fish fillets; breaded, partially cooked and frozen) | 4 sticks |

## Vegetables

Here's a guide-at-a-glance to help you buy vegetables wisely and in season.

Buy fresh vegetables that are bright in color and crisp with no sign of decay.

Buy vegetables in the quantity you can use without waste or for which you have refrigerator storage space for 2 to 5 days. Root vegetables can be bought in larger amounts.

### Seasonal Buying Guide

| Vegetables | Peak Season |
|---|---|
| Artichokes | October to June |
| Asparagus | March to July |
| Beans | May to November |
| Beets | June to November |
| Broccoli | October to May |
| Brussels sprouts | September to March |
| Cabbage | All year |
| Carrots | All year |
| Cauliflower | September to May |
| Celery | All year |
| Chinese cabbage | All year |
| Corn, sweet | May to October |
| Cucumbers | All year |
| Eggplant | All year |
| Endive and escarole | All year |
| Garlic | All year |
| Lettuce and other greens | All year |
| Mushrooms | All year |
| Okra | May to October |
| Onions | All year |
| Parsley and herbs | All year |
| Parsnips | All year |
| Peas | February to September |
| Peppers | All year |
| Potatoes | All year |
| Pumpkins | September and October |
| Radishes | All year |
| Spinach | January to July |
| Sweet potatoes and squash | All year |
| Tomatoes | All year |
| Turnips and rutabagas | September to April |

# Storing Foods

Do you know why you shouldn't store foods near the dishwasher? How to refrigerate egg yolks properly? Why you should thaw frozen cheese in the refrigerator? Whether pineapples will ripen during storage? If you can freeze cottage cheese? How and how long to store dry foods? Some of the answers may surprise you.

## Shelf Storage (Room Temperature)

Store dry foods in their original wrappings or in airtight containers after opening. Tight storage containers also help keep out insects.

Store foods in cool kitchen cabinets. Do not store in areas over the range or near the dishwasher or refrigerator exhaust, because these locations are too warm for long shelf life.

### Guidelines for Shelf Storage

| Foods | Length of Time | Storage Precautions |
|---|---|---|
| **Breads, Cereals, Flours** | | |
| Breads, rolls | 5 to 7 days | Store in tightly closed original package; refrigerate in hot weather. |
| Cake mixes | 1 year | |
| Cereals, ready-to-cook | 4 to 6 months | |
|     ready-to-eat | 3 months | Reseal flap after opening to keep crisp. |
| Cookies, packaged | 4 months | Store in tightly closed container. |
| Crackers | 3 months | Same as cookies. |
| Crumbs, dry bread or cracker | 6 months | |
| Flour, all-purpose | 1 year | Store in tightly closed container. |
| Main dish mixes | 1 year | |
| Noodles, egg | 6 months | |
| Pancake mixes | 6 months | |
| Pasta | 1 year | |
| Pie crust mixes | 6 months | |
| Rice, brown or wild | 6 months | Use seasoned mixes within 6 months. |
|     white | 1 year | |
| Sugar, brown or powdered | 4 months | |
|     granulated | 2 years | |
| **Beverages** | | |
| Coffee, instant | 6 months | |
|     vacuum pack | 1 year | Refrigerate after opening. |
| Tea, bags or loose | 6 months | |
|     instant | 1 year | |
| Wine (unopened) | Depends on vintage (year and country). | Store bottle on its side in dark place at 55°F. |
| Wine (opened) | See Refrigerator Storage on page 150. | |
| **Canned Foods** | | |
| All kinds | 1 year | Date the cans; use oldest first. |

## Guidelines for Shelf Storage

| Foods | Length of Time | Storage Precautions |
| --- | --- | --- |
| **Condiments** | | |
| Catsup, chili sauce | 1 month | Refrigerate after opening. |
| **Dairy** | | |
| Milk, nonfat dry | 2 months | |
|   whole dry | 2 weeks | Refrigerate after opening. |
| Parmesan cheese, grated | 1 month | |
| **Fats, Oils** | | |
| Cooking or salad | 3 months | Refrigerate after opening. |
| Lard (stabilized by hydrogenation or anti-oxidants) | 8 months | Refrigerate lard that is not stabilized. |
| Mayonnaise, salad dressings | 3 months | Refrigerate after opening. |
| Shortening, hydrogenated | 8 months | |
| **Fruits** | | |
| Dried | 6 months | |
| Fresh | Store at room temperature until ripe. | Refrigerate when ripe. |
| **Leavenings, Seasonings, Herbs, Spices** | | |
| Baking powder, baking soda | 18 months | Buy in small amounts and date the containers. |
| Bouillon, cubes or instant | 1 year | |
| Herbs and spices, ground | 6 months | Date the containers. |
|   whole | 1 year | Same as ground. |
| **Miscellaneous** | | |
| Frostings, canned | 8 months | Refrigerate after opening. |
| Gelatin, plain or flavored | 18 months | |
| Honey, jams, syrups | 1 year | Refrigerate syrups after opening. |
| Molasses | 2 years | |
| Olives, pickles | 1 year | Refrigerate after opening. |
| Peanut butter (unopened) | 6 months | |
| Peanut butter (opened) | See Refrigerator Storage on page 152. | |
| Pudding mixes | 1 year | |
| Sauce mixes, gravy mixes, soup mixes | 6 months | |
| Whipped topping mixes | 1 year | |
| **Vegetables** | | |
| Root type | 1 week | Store longer at 45° to 50°F in a dry, dark place. (See Refrigerator Storage on page 152.) |

# Refrigerator Storage (40°F)

Keep refrigerator temperature at 40°F or slightly lower. Always store produce in plastic bags or containers with tight-fitting lids to retain moisture and prevent transfer of odors to other foods. Remove foods from refrigerator only when you are ready to cook or serve them.

## Guidelines for Refrigerator Storage

| Foods | Length of Time | Storage Precautions |
|---|---|---|
| **Breads, Cereals, Flours** | | |
| Breads | 5 to 7 days | Refrigerate during summer. |
| Cakes with frosting, pies with cream or custard fillings | 2 days | Refrigerate until serving time. |
| Flour, whole-grain or rye | 1 year | Store in tightly closed container. |
| **Beverages** | | |
| Coffee (opened) | 1 week | Whole coffee beans will keep longer than ground coffee. |
| Wine (opened) | 1 to 2 days | Pour remaining wine into a smaller container so there's less contact with air. Refrigerate white wine; store red airtight at room temperature. |
| **Condiments** | | |
| Barbecue sauce, horseradish | 1 month | |
| **Dairy** | | |
| Buttermilk, dairy sour cream, yogurt | 2 weeks | Check the freshness date on the container before purchase. |
| Cheese, cottage | 3 to 5 days | Refrigerate tightly covered. |
| cream | 2 weeks | |
| hard | 2 months | Wrap tightly; discard if moldy. |
| sliced | 2 weeks | |
| spread | 1 to 2 weeks | Refrigerate covered after opening. |
| Cream | 3 to 5 days | Refrigerate tightly closed. |
| Milk, reconstituted dry | 5 days | Refrigerate evaporated and condensed tightly covered after opening. |
| skim | 5 days | |
| whole | 5 days | |
| **Eggs** | | |
| Dried | 1 year | Refrigerate in airtight container. |
| Fresh | 1 week | Can be refrigerated longer, but expect loss of some quality and flavor. |
| Yolks, whites | 2 to 4 days | Cover yolks with cold water. Refrigerate yolks and whites covered. |

## Guidelines for Refrigerator Storage

| Foods | Length of Time | Storage Precautions |
|---|---|---|
| **Fats, Oils** | | |
| Butter | 2 weeks | Refrigerate tightly covered. |
| Margarine | 1 month | |
| Mayonnaise, salad dressings | 3 months | Refrigerate after opening. |
| **Fruits** | | |
| Apples | 1 month | Refrigerate ripe apples uncovered. |
| Apricots, avocados, grapes, melons, peaches, pears, plums | 3 to 5 days | Store at room temperature until ripe and then refrigerate. |
| Bananas | 3 to 5 days | Skin on bananas will darken in refrigerator. |
| Berries, cherries | 2 to 3 days | Do not wash or remove stems before refrigerating. |
| Cranberries | 1 week | Refrigerate covered. |
| Citrus | 2 weeks | Store uncovered in refrigerator. |
| Dried | 6 months | Refrigerate during hot, humid weather. |
| Juice, reconstituted frozen | 2 days | Refrigerate covered in glass or plastic container. |
| Pineapple | 2 to 3 days | Use soon after purchase; no further ripening occurs during storage. |
| **Meats, Poultry, Seafood** | | |
| Meats, fresh | | Cover lightly and refrigerate. |
| chops | 2 to 3 days | |
| ground | 1 day | |
| roasts | 2 to 3 days | |
| steaks | 2 to 3 days | |
| variety | 1 day | |
| Meats, processed | | |
| cold cuts (unopened) | 2 weeks | |
| cold cuts (opened) | 3 to 5 days | |
| cured, bacon | 1 week | |
| frankfurters | 1 week | |
| ham, canned | | |
| (unopened) | 1 year | |
| half | 5 days | |
| slices | 3 days | |
| whole | 1 week | |
| Poultry and seafood | 1 to 2 days | Refrigerate in plastic wrap or waxed paper. |

## Guidelines for Refrigerator Storage

| Foods | Length of Time | Storage Precautions |
|---|---|---|
| **Miscellaneous** | | |
| Coffee lighteners | 3 weeks | Refrigerate after thawing. |
| Cooked dishes | 3 to 4 days | Cover and refrigerate promptly. |
| Gravy, broth | 1 to 2 days | Cover and refrigerate promptly. |
| Nuts, shelled | 3 months | Refrigerate in airtight containers; also can be frozen. Unshelled nuts can be stored at room temperature. |
| Peanut butter (opened) | 2 months | |
| Pickles, olives | 1 month | |
| Stuffing | 1 to 2 days | Remove from fowl; refrigerate immediately. |
| **Vegetables** | | |
| Asparagus | 2 to 3 days | Do not wash before refrigerating. |
| Broccoli, Brussels sprouts, green onions, summer squash | 3 to 5 days | Store in refrigerator crisper, plastic bags or containers. |
| Cabbage, carrots, parsnips, radishes, rutabagas | 2 weeks | Remove tops of root vegetables; refrigerate in plastic bags. |
| Cauliflower, celery, cucumbers, eggplant, green beans, green peppers | 1 week | Store in refrigerator crisper, plastic bags or containers. |
| Corn, sweet | 1 day | Refrigerate unhusked and uncovered. |
| Green peas, lima beans | 3 to 5 days | Refrigerate in pods. |
| Lettuce, greens | 5 to 7 days | Wash and drain well; refrigerate in crisper. Produce stored in vacuum pack containers (airproof) lasts 3 to 6 times longer. |
| Onions, dry | 2 months | Store in open mesh containers in cool, dry room. |
| Potatoes | 2 months | Store in well-ventilated, dark, dry place at 45° to 50°F. Stored at room temperature, they will keep about a week. |
| Sweet potatoes, winter squash | 2 months | Store at about 60°F. |
| Tomatoes | 1 week | Keep at room temperature and away from direct sunlight until ripe. Refrigerate uncovered. |

# Freezer Storage (0°F)

Keep freezer temperature at 0°F or lower. Wrap food in moisture/vaporproof materials to retain flavor, moisture and nutrients, and remove as much air from packages as possible.

Remember to label and date all packages and use the longest-stored food first. Foods that are purchased frozen should be kept frozen in original packages. When thawing frozen meats, poultry, fish and seafood, allow enough time to defrost them in refrigerator.

## Guidelines for Freezer Storage

| Foods | Length of Time | Storage Precautions |
| --- | --- | --- |
| **Breads, Cereals, Flours** | | |
| Breads, baked | 2 to 3 months | |
| unbaked | 3 weeks | |
| Cakes, baked | 3 to 4 months | |
| frosted | 2 to 3 months | |
| Cookies, baked | 3 to 4 months | Package in small amounts. |
| Doughnuts, quick breads | 2 to 3 months | |
| Pies, baked | 4 months | Do not freeze custard or cream pies or pies with a meringue topping. |
| unbaked pie shells | 2 months | |
| baked pie shells | 4 months | |
| Sandwiches | 1 month | Wrap tightly; freeze individually. |
| **Dairy** | | |
| Cheese, natural or process | 3 to 4 months | Creamed cottage cheese and cream cheese are not recommended for freezing. Freeze other cheeses in small amounts and thaw in refrigerator to prevent crumbling. |
| Cream, heavy | 2 to 3 months | Texture changes, but it can be whipped after thawing. |
| Ice cream, sherbet | 1 month | Cover surface with foil to reduce formation of ice crystals. |
| Milk | 3 to 4 months | Freeze in original carton. |
| **Eggs** | | |
| Fresh | not recommended | |
| Whites | 1 year | Use promptly after thawing. |
| Yolks | 3 months | Special care needed; see page 50. |
| **Fats, Oils** | | |
| Butter, margarine | 4 to 6 months | |
| **Fruits** | | |
| Home frozen, commercial | 8 to 12 months | Wrap, label and date package. |

## Guidelines for Freezer Storage

| Foods | Length of Time | Storage Precautions |
|---|---|---|
| **Meat, Poultry, Seafood, Fish** | | |
| Beef, roasts or steaks | 8 to 12 months | |
|   ground or stew | 2 to 3 months | |
| Fish, breaded, cooked | 2 to 3 months | |
|   fatty | 3 to 4 months | |
|   lean | 6 to 8 months | |
| Game birds, ducks or geese | 6 to 8 months | |
| Lamb, roasts or steaks | 8 to 12 months | |
| Meats, cooked | 1 to 3 months | |
| Pork, bacon | 1 month | Freeze bacon and frankfurters in vacuum wrap and overwrap for storage longer than 2 weeks. |
|   cured | 1 to 2 months | Cured pork loses desirable color and flavor during freezer storage. |
|   frankfurters | 2 months | |
|   fresh roasts | 4 to 6 months | |
| Poultry, cooked | | |
|   creamed | 3 to 4 months | |
|   no sauce | 1 month | Wrap airtight; it dries out quickly. |
| Poultry, uncooked | | |
|   cut up | 4 to 6 months | |
|   giblets | 1 to 3 months | |
|   whole | 6 to 8 months | |
| Seafood, lobster or scallops | 1 to 2 months | |
|   shellfish | 3 to 4 months | |
| Turkey rolls | 6 months | Purchase solidly frozen and freeze in original wrapping. |
| Variety meats | 1 to 2 months | |
| Veal, roasts, steaks | 4 to 8 months | |
| **Miscellaneous** | | |
| Juices, fruit | 1 year | |
| Leftover main dishes | 1 month | |
| Nuts, shelled | 3 months | |
| Stews, soups | 2 to 3 months | |
| **Vegetables** | | |
| Home frozen | 8 to 12 months | |
| Commercial | 8 months | |

# Safety in the Kitchen

Good safety practices and strict cleanliness have top priority in the kitchen for hazard-free cooking and freedom from foodborne illnesses.

## Cooking Equipment and Utensils

▸ To unplug appliances for cleaning, pull plug, never the appliance cord.

▸ Always dry hands before touching an electrical switch or plug.

▸ Turn off mixer and unplug it before inserting or removing beaters.

▸ Turn off blender or food processor before scraping sides of container.

▸ Use kitchen tongs to remove cooking pouches from boiling water; cut pouches open with kitchen scissors.

▸ Always lift covers from hot pans up and away from you to avoid burns from steam.

▸ Use great care when handling knives by keeping a firm grip on the handle and turning the sharp edge away from you and your hand when chopping or paring foods. Rest hand firmly on French knife tip on cutting board. Lift knife handle up and down across food, chopping to desired size.

## Food Handling

▸ Keep your kitchen sanitary by cleaning surfaces, crevices on counters, appliances, equipment and utensils with soap and water or with a cleanser.

▸ Prepare raw meat or poultry on plastic cutting boards, which are easily cleaned. If you use wooden cutting boards, clean the surface with a solution of 1 teaspoon chlorine bleach and ½ teaspoon vinegar to 2 quarts of water.

▸ Wash hands thoroughly with soap and water. Do not handle food if your hands have cuts or sores.

▸ Wash all containers before using to store, cook or serve meat or poultry.

▸ To avoid transferring germs from raw meat to cooked meat, never use the same dishes for preparation and serving without washing them thoroughly between steps.

▸ Wash the crisper drawer of your refrigerator often and keep containers for storing refrigerated food very clean.

## Hot and Cold Foods

▸ Keep hot foods hot (above 140°F) and cold foods cold (below 40°F) to control organisms that can cause food spoilage. Do not let any food, cold or hot, stand at room temperature for more than 2 hours; bacteria grow best in lukewarm food.

▸ Use special care with perishable foods containing eggs, milk, seafood, meat and poultry (such as creamed foods, poultry or seafood salads and cream pies) where there is a possibility of food spoilage.

▸ Cook ground meat thoroughly and never eat raw ground meat. It's not safe.

▸ Cook ham according to label directions; some hams are not precooked and should be cooked to 160°F.

▸ Reduce the temperature of large quantities of hot food quickly by placing the cooking container in a sink filled with cold water and ice; refrigerate promptly when tepid.

▸ Serve perishable foods in moderate-size serving dishes for a buffet. Refill often so that food is kept cold or hot as long as possible.

▸ Refrigerate food in containers that can be brought directly to the table. Use insulated dishes to help keep foods cold or hot.

# Index

# Index